CHERISH THE LIGHT
One Woman's Journey from Darkness to Light

Thoughts about Donna

Oprah Winfrey introduced Donna Friess and previewed her story on *The Oprah Winfrey Show* stating, "This is a story of power and unbelievable perversion…It was the cover story in the *Los Angeles Times Magazine.* This is a show you cannot afford not to watch!" Oprah Winfrey, television celebrity and social activist.

"Dr. Donna Friess is the most inspirational person I have ever met. She imparts a divine influence on the mind and soul." Jack H., Former student, certificated drug and alcohol counselor.

"Donna is solid gold. She is good and brave and willing to share. She is the blessing of God, too bright to behold for those of us who love misery (too many of us, I am afraid). She has taught me so much!" Lisa Williams

"Twenty-two years ago when I was a student in Donna's class she planted a seed in my heart and showed me how special I was. Because of her inspiration and wisdom, I have become a successful coach and am loving life. Her influence on my life has been profound!" Marylou H., Life Coach

"Donna Friess turned her hurt into a halo, her scars into stars, what an inspiration she is to all!!!" Rev. Robert Schuller, Founder of Crystal Cathedral, National figure in television ministry.

Dr. Donna Friess has utilized a horrible childhood life experience and family tragedy as her driving force to help the nation's incest victims. Dr. Friess is a friend and advisor to hundreds of victims and students. She is an inspiration to thousands, a wonderful fun-loving motivational speaker who enjoys surfing and playing with her grandchildren. I am very proud and fortunate to call Donna Friess my friend." Collene Thompson Campbell, Former Mayor, San Juan Capistrano, National Institute of Corrections, Appointed by the U.S. Attorney General.

Comments about *Cry the Darkness*

"A real contribution to women everywhere." *Changes Magazine.*

"It is a wonderful book!" Marilyn Van Derbur, Former Miss America, incest survivor.

"I couldn't put it down. It is inspirational!" *Alpha Gamma Delta International Quarterly*

"It is a gripping story…it keeps the reader moving." U.S. International University, *Envoy.*

"A must read for everyone. One of the most important books available. It gives hope. Donna's life story is a beacon of hope and happiness for adult survivors of sexual abuse." Claire Reeves, Founder, Mothers Against Sexual Abuse.

Cry the Darkness is my most valued possession." Gina, Incest survivor and AIDS patient.

"I learned that I was not alone." Lydia, Mother whose daughter was an incest victim.

"An inspiration for those working for victims of childhood trauma." *Changes Magazine*

"Outstanding Donna, A good reminder that we DO have a choice in how we respond." Judy P., Reader.

"Wonderful sharing and my wish and prayers sent to Donna for continued courage as she moves through the process and examination of the past as it has blended with the future…..thanks to her for having such courage and how it has helped so many. Years ago, I still remember when I read in the LA Times about her and her family's ordeal exposing this family secret….as I remember it was in the LA Times…I sure thought atta girl then and still do now." Sharon A.

Reviews: *Circle of Love: Guide to Successful Relationships*

"It is possible to take control of your life. It is possible to change. It is possible to become more like the person you always wanted to be. Dr. Friess provides a path for you to achieve what you want." Jun K. Student.

"Great book! One of the best interactive self help books available. Halfway through it, I bought copies for my family and friends." Jennifer H., Student.

"Dr. Friess is an amazing woman and her book reflects her unique ability to teach others how to develop, maintain, and enhance relationships. Her suggestions guide people to be more satisfied with their lived. I know my life has been significantly influenced by Dr. Friess. I will forever be grateful." Christy S, Student.

Circle of Love is a well written book filled with insight and compassion for the human soul. Each chapter highlights a vital ingredient for success in communication. It encourages the reader to respond honestly without guilt. I value each lesson learned! I will continue to use the tools and reference for success in my life." Julie P. Mother, Re-entry Student.

"This book changed my life!" William F., Single parent.

Other Books by Donna Friess

Cry the Darkness: One Woman's Triumph over the Tragedy of Incest, Updated & Re-released, 2013

Cry the Darkness: One Woman's Triumph over the Tragedy of Incest, 1993

Circle of Love: A Guide to Successful Relationships, 3rd Edition

One Hundred Years of Weesha: Centennial 2010

Whispering Waters: Historic Weesha and the Settling of Southern California
With Janet Tonkovich

A Chronicle of Historic Weesha and the Upper Santa Ana River Valley
With Janet Tonkovich

Just Between Us: Guide to Healing (out of print)

True Animal Short Stories for Children:

Oh What a Big Surprise!

Three Little Kittens Lost in the Woodpile

Zoe's First Birthday

There's Something Scary in the Shed

Starving in the Woods

Winning the Horse Race

Jessica the Seal

CHERISH THE LIGHT

One Woman's Journey from Darkness to Light

DONNA L. FRIESS, PH.D.

HURT INTO HAPPINESS PUBLISHING
San Juan Capistrano, California

Library of Congress-in-Publication Data

All Rights Reserved
Copyright 2013 Donna L. Friess

Friess, Donna L.
Cherish the Light: One Woman's Journey from Darkness to Light

Donna L. Friess
Includes bibliographical references.
Biography

Hurt into Happiness Publishing 2013
32332 Camino Capistrano, Suite 102, San Juan Capistrano, CA 92675

ISBN-13 978-0-9815767-2-5
ISBN-10 9815767-2-9

Front cover designed by Diana Starr with Donna's oil painting of granddaughter, Jaycelin, as she cherished a ray of light one day in Avalon, CA.

Visit: www.drdonnafriess.com and www.yourtimenow.org to order books or go to Amazon.com. Also available as Ebook through Kindle Publishing and Nook.

ACKNOWLEDGMENTS

I am grateful to my husband Ken for his constant support and good sense in editing my various manuscripts. He truly is the wind beneath my wings. Thank you to the early readers for your excellent feedback: Julina Bert, Mary Berberich, Lisa Williams, Ginni Condi, and Ken Friess. A special thank you to Lisa Williams for her skillful editing. My sister Diana Starr's technical support, as well as her creativity in terms of cover design and editing, have allowed me to reach higher than ever.

It is the openness and heartfelt sharing on the part of my friends, students, colleagues, clients, and group participants that has permitted me a more clear view into the human condition. Your naked honesty has helped to expand my thinking beyond my own experience. I appreciate you deeply. I am humbled by your trust in me.

I attribute a great deal of who I have become to the great minds which have so heavily influenced me. If not for their efforts to write down their beliefs, thoughts, and feelings, or share them in seminars, I would not have had the benefit of their thinking. You will discover my appreciation for them in the pages of this book.

If I were not surrounded by a constant flow of love from my husband, children, mother, family, and friends, none of this would be possible.

For my children, my grandchildren and those

Great-grandchildren who are yet unborn;

You inspire me to Cherish the Light; to

Count each blessing.

TABLE OF CONTENTS

INTRODUCTION

"What lies behind us and what lies before us are tiny matters compared to what lies within us."
Unknown

When I sat down to write <u>Cry the Darkness</u>, I could not help but replay the awful scene that so easily flashed across my memory. The book begins with: *"I couldn't watch when they brought him into the courtroom in shackles, but I know I'll hear the sound of those chains for the rest of my life. How could I bear seeing my father restrained like some mad dog?"*

I was wrong about that. It has been 23 years and I have not thought much about those chains at all. Even his vicious warnings across my childhood, *"Sorry sisters end up six feet under"* is becoming more dim in my memory. It feels like a dream in many ways, that my childhood was a nightmare of abuse and control; that I worked myself free of it only to learn in midlife that dad was molesting our three-year-old old niece. There was no one else to stop him. I risked my marriage, career, our standing in the community, and my actual life to stop him from doing to her what he had done to all of his daughters and a granddaughter. It simply had to stop and it did. But back then, in the middle of that awful 15 month long trial, I could not imagine what my future could bring. I had hunkered down in survival mode.

Life today is rich and lively in a way I never dreamed possible when I wrote: *"The secret that I'd kept buried for a lifetime might have gone with me to the grave, but now I knew that my father hadn't stopped. He wouldn't stop until someone stopped him."* So much has changed, not just in my internal world, but in my external world as well. I have traveled from a dark secret to transparency and light. No longer do I live in the cozy nuclear family of husband Ken, myself, and three children. Today we live in the midst of a big, noisy, sprawling family. There are horses in the backyard, three Golden Retrievers, and five cats under foot, with grandkids dropping in at random times for a swim.

FOREWORD

To have the same best friend for 57 years is quite something. When I first met Donna at 14 years of age, I chose her as dance partner because the girl she was with was too tall for me. We have been dancing together ever since.

If you do not already know my wife, you will find that she likes to dance to many different types of music. She writes like she dances, always with happiness, vigor, and a special grace, but you do not always know what to expect. I have learned to "go with the flow" when we dance, and really, as we have lived our lives. When you read this book, I would ask you to do the same.

Donna misses very few of life's details and has an incredible memory for them. She also has an ability to ferret out the good in a sea of bad things. She does not deny there are bad events and bad people, she simply chooses thriving, and is determined to find joy. She does this not through denial, but through confrontation and choice.

This book has been created as a tapestry of her experiences. It is a look at lives "well lived" and is filled with thought provoking ideas and science. As you read it, allow yourself to "go with the flow." You are embarking on a journey that should, at a minimum, be pleasant, and could well be life changing. There is no question my dance partner changed my life for the better.

Ken Friess
San Juan Capistrano, CA

PROLOGUE

"The best things in life aren't things."
Art Buchwald

August 15, 2012
Boardwalk
Santa Cruz, CA.

"Mimi you want a leg up?" Asked my strapping 17 year-old grandson Jake as he boosted me onto the carousel horse of my choice, a shiny white beauty mounted strategically on the outside lane, all the better for grabbing the brass ring! A wave of pleasure pulsed through me as I admired her ruby eyes. She reminded me of my pony, at home, Pixie, and of course, of a long ago favorite carousel horse when I was a child. This was so much fun! I was glad that I had flown to Oakland to meet up with Julie and her boys to check out universities with Jake.

"Jake, great. I'm set!" I was up and readied myself to grasp the rings as we whirled by. James and Julie were on the horses in front of me and Jake was just behind. We were lined up as sentries determined to get those rings, all of us sporting eager smiles. I snapped a few photos and secured the camera around my neck. The organ music started and our horses began to move, slowly at first, but gaining speed with each rotation. We could hear the clacking of the rings as they loaded into the delivery shaft. We were off! I watched as Julie successfully plucked her first ring, then James, who missed his, then it was my turn. Out went my determined fingers, but I missed. Around we went again gaining more speed. Julie yanked and then tossed her ring at the waiting clown's face. Next was James; successful this time. Jubilant. Then my turn. I grabbed it. I was so elated that I forgot to toss it at the clown. Around and around we went, faster and faster. I managed to nab a ring and then toss it. I was heady with triumph, so much so that I was barely ready when my turn came again. I missed.

This time Julie managed to get her ring into the much smaller target of the clown's open mouth. A victory! Julie bellowed out her joyous success.

Whirling and grabbing, smiling and laughing, around we went. With each cycle my brain spun backward to my seven year-old arm stretching out as far as possible, ready to clasp the same kind of ring. It was the Ocean Park Pier of my childhood. The 1940's, and still the hay days of the waterfront amusement piers up and down the west coast. In full view of my memory, I could almost smell the cotton candy and hear the delighted squeals of the children mixed with the canned laughter of the two Laffing Sals who welcomed guests to the famous seaside park. Sandy would be behind me, frantic to grab a ring. We rode the merry-go-round so often in those days but catching the coveted brass ring and getting a free ride was still a much sought after event.

I was reliving a Sunday of my childhood. Sandy and I would have walked from the tiny beach cottage where we lived to Muscle Beach in Venice. I was holding her hand to keep her safe. I would have paid the 5 cents which it cost each of us to ride the tram from Venice to Ocean Park where we would have checked in with our champion checker-playing grandfather, Big Ray. He would have looked up and smiled his toothless grin, introduced us to his fellow checker players, reached into his dark suit pocket and retrieved some coins for us. There would have been a hug exchanged and then Sandy and I would have scampered off, free to ride the carousel for the next few hours. The checker players would have gone back to trying to beat "Doc" at his game. In those days, he was famous with the checker playing set of Los Angeles.

Smiling from that sweet memory, I came back to the present moment, (not so different from those of 60 years ago,) but now I was the grandparent and the children were my grandchildren. But I was not playing checkers, I was after the brass ring!

I laughed to myself, surely I had won it. It had to be the brass ring to have raised such a beautiful healthy family and decades later be playing the same kinds of amusements with them that I had so enjoyed. The Long Beach Pike, Ocean Park Pier, Santa Monica Pier, Santa Cruz Boardwalk, Playland in San Francisco; what delicious memories! Hot blueberry pie in San Francisco after Sandy and I had rolled and rolled in the tumbling tunnel of the fun house. Delectable frozen "cream" at the Arctic ice cream parlor in another, adrenaline-charged whoops on all the roller coasters up and down the coast. Those fun zones had a magic of their own.

The trademark of that bygone era, before Walt Disney got his big idea, had to be those iconic Laffing Sals. From 1930-1950 three hundred of them welcomed guests across the country. The stout animated feminine figures sported a gap-tooth smile, giggled and gyrated to attract patrons long before the Disney animated characters were born. The raucous cackling from the Sal at Ocean Park was all it took to turn on my own giggle machine. I could not walk past her without breaking into my own delighted squeals. Just thinking about it still cracks me up; she never stopped, she just laughed and laughed and laughed!

I love that the Santa Cruz Boardwalk exhibits one of the very last Sals in existence. In a way it feels like visiting a piece of my own past. The Sals have not been seen much since the 50's. The fun zone beach parks have mostly disappeared over time, victims of storm damage and social change; but this one in Santa Cruz boasts that it is the only one on the whole of the west coast that has been in continuous operation. Today it has two gigantic roller coasters, arcades, aerial trams, whirly rides and of course bumper cars.

The bell clanged and the carousel slowed down and came to a stop. As we climbed off our horses, Julie entertained us with the details of her victorious toss into the clown's actual mouth. Jake proudly reported that he caught a ring on each turn, and James smiled as he said, "So Mom, I'm ready for that dessert now, maybe dippin' dots ice cream."

"Not until I get you guys at bumper cars!" challenged Jake.

"I'm up for it!" I chimed in.

Bumper cars! I feared that my dear Jake was in for a jolt to his "world view" regarding his Mimi, me. My wonderful boy had no idea what was in store for him when he challenged us and climbed into his shiny blue bumper car. The starting buzzer sounded and the electric floor became "hot." I could see Jake in front of me a few cars up. I slipped around a green car, gained speed and WHAM! I quickly crashed into the back of him. Shocked, he turned around to see that it was me, his gleeful grandmother laughing like a maniac as I raced away to the safety at the perimeter of the floor. I turned for a quick glimpse and saw that he was in hot pursuit. I swerved between a few little kids in slower cars and kept to the edge. Jake's face was all determination as he gunned it. He was coming for me but suddenly the congestion in front of him forced him to slow down. I made a quick get-away! I kept my wits about me and slipped between the colorful cars until I was behind him yet again. Wham! You could almost see him thinking *What? Not again?* Our family is nothing if not competitive. With an even more resolute set to his shoulders he took off in full pursuit but by now I was way in front of him. Around and around the floor we chased each other. I could tell that he *really* wanted to get a shot at me, but I was too slippery. I am sure he was thinking that there is no way this grandmother is going to get the best of me! I kept to the edges of the floor and then like a stealthful guerilla warrior I emerged from the cover of the other cars to strike him yet again! He tried his hardest to reciprocate but I was too fast and too sneaky. The ending clang sounded. Ha Ha. My childhood strategy of cruising the periphery until my target was within range paid off.

During all the zooming around that electric floor, an old memory came to me about how much Dad had loved the bumping cars. Actually he had been quite a devotee of all such amusements, and by our teens my sister Sandy and I, with our Dad leading the charge, had visited all of the major amusement attractions in the United States. We did this during our various treks across the country with camping trailer in tow. They were good memories. Happy memories. It was always best for me to stay in that mental place.

As we concluded our visit and continued down the boardwalk, Julie linked her arm affectionately around Jake's neck. James put his arm around my waist as Jake summed up the afternoon, "Well Mims, I had no idea that you had a secret life as a commando. That was some fancy car bumping. Lady, there is NO way this is over! There is going to be a rematch and watch out! I'm going to devote my full energies to practicing so I can whomp you next time!" teased Jake, his light green eyes dancing with merriment.

"Hey, so who is ready to head south and explore Big Sur?" asked Jake. "During the drive here while the Mimster was obviously scheming about bumping cars, I found a really awesome waterfall in the California guide book. I think we should hike to it. It's 75 feet tall and the fresh water cascades onto the beach!"

With that we were off on another part of our adventure, and I knew that I was enjoying the best adventure of all; sharing these precious moments of this check-out-the-universities-road trip with my daughter and grandsons.

As Julie's SUV headed south on Highway 1, my memory kept coming back to that delightful amusement pier. In a way I grew up around so many of them. I had loved the Ocean Park Pier, which was right by our house. I remembered that in the late 50's it was sold and became Pacific Ocean Park. It was very popular while I was in high school, and then somehow, over the years while I was raising my family, it was boarded up and eventually torn down, and I never thought much about it.

That image brought me to another memory of another boarded up pier. When I was a kid a beautiful pier stood at the end of Venice Boulevard from 1921-1946. The Red Car was a street car that deposited thousands of eager beachgoers to the foot of the Venice Pier all summer long. It ran from downtown L.A. to the beach.

When I was a young child that pier still stood; closed-up but still present and situated next to the playground where our mother was a recreation leader. I have dozens of photographs of my great-grandparents and my grandmother Maymie posing in front of it. It had always intrigued me as in some ways it seemed to contain a mythical ghostly vibe of my long ago ancestors, but during my days it was but an ancient relic.

Suddenly a long ago memory transported me to a hot summer day. Our mother was tending the playground where she worked not 100 yards from that pier. Sandy and I had the job of keeping out of the way. On this particular day an older girl with a nervous little dog, dared Sandy and me to go into the closed down pier.

"We're not supposed to leave the playground." I responded in a worried voice.

"Well, we'll just be gone for a minute. Your mom won't even know you're gone. She's busy with that carom tournament. Come on! Or are you a yellow chicken?"

Not one to easily back down, I agreed to go, but just to look. Taking Sandy by the hand, we sneaked up the ramp into the pier and slid in between two loose boards. It was spooky. It was so dark down below that you could barely see the white foam of the waves, but the moans as the surf crashed into the pilings were eerie. One false step and certain death lay below.

We traveled a little further out onto the pier. We must have been inside some kind of old structure, maybe an old fun house. The malignant moans of the waves continued; crashing and receding. Suddenly the older girl raced across the single plank stretched precariously over a wide space. I took her dare, but soon realized it was a bad decision. My child's terrified voice still rang in my memory as I yelled to Sandy, "Stay back. This is scary. Sandy, stay back!"

I imagined what could have happened had I fallen into the dark waters below. What if Sandy had followed me across? She was so little. I remember that we raced out of there and ran back to the safety of our corner of the sand box. We stayed there for a long time, each of us lost in our own thoughts. Later our mom came looking for us. We never told her about our terrible adventure. It was our dangerous little secret.

From the back seat Jake handed me the guide book as he said, "So Mimi here is that picture of the falls I want us to see."

With that I turned my attention back to the present. As I leafed through the pages of the guide book, I thought how lucky I was to be traveling with the kids like this, to be a part of this giant-sized family and to be enjoying the past mixed with the present. I understood that my choices had led me here to this moment and this life but it could all have gone so horribly wrong. One missed step and as dad always said, "Sorry sisters end up six-feet-under." I refused to go to the place where I thought about the scars left deep within my psyche, the residue from years of living under my father's reign of terror.

I thought about my new life; all the children, my wonderful husband, my beloved Golden Retrievers, my life coaching practice and the grief counseling work. Ever since *Cry the Darkness* came out 20 years ago, audiences have badgered me to know the secrets of how I have succeeded in having a happy life. Even today, my clients continue to ask, "Donna explain how you have managed not to live as a victim? How do you stay so focused on the positive in life? You are the most joyful and positive person we know. How have you done it?"

How indeed? Good question.

SECTION ONE: BREAKING FREE OF THE DARK

WELCOME

Welcome dear reader to my reflections. It has been more than 20 years since the agony of discovering that my father had not stopped hurting the girls in the family. That was a dark time for me. During the years since, as friends, associates, clients, and listeners have come to know me, when they see the zest for life that oozes out of my pores, they often pull me aside and whisper these questions: "Donna tell me how you did it? How can a person have been neglected and abused and end up the way you are? How did you manage to progress from victim to the flourishing woman we see today?" I have thought long and hard about that and I invite you on a journey, a little expedition through my thoughts. The road might not always be perfectly straight as simultaneous events in life are shared with you. Bring your detective equipment and look for clues along the way, while I share my heart with you. I suspect that by the end of our time together I will have learned something new about myself, and perhaps there is something in my attitudes, actions and experiences which will resonate with you. Come with me now.

Our story begins in the summer of 1993. That year had a lot of parts to it. In addition to my full time teaching schedule, I completed my doctoral degree and enjoyed a May graduation. Ken, who was not to be out done by his wife, [there was not going to be "Mr. and Dr. Donna Friess" at our house], was completing his Ph.D. as well, while he ran his construction company. The same day as my ceremony, Dan, our youngest son, graduated with his bachelor's degree from UCSD. He was accepted into a Master's program in engineering at Berkeley. Rick, our oldest son, was working full time as an attorney and had met a beautiful paralegal from his law firm. Julie, our daughter, and I were teaching full time and enjoying having the summer off to prepare for her wedding. My book, Cry the Darkness was released in May and I had the privilege of seeing it in our local bookstores. It was a busy time.

CHAPTER ONE: A POPULATION EXPLOSION AT FRIESS HAUS

"If we aren't supposed to dance, why all the music?"
Gregory Orr

May 11, 2012
San Juan Capistrano, CA.

If there is such a thing as past life, I bet I was an historian, or maybe that's the plan for the next one? Wouldn't it be neat if we had multiple lives? All I know is that I am forever making people look at the camera, "Smile" as I bug them to let me take a photo. Also, I am frequently pulling out the camcorder for action shots. I have dozens of big color Shutterfly books, photo albums and videos capturing special memories. I'm saving them for when I am old and have time to look at them! I am happy for this particular compulsion because today I wanted to refresh my memory about the summer of our daughter, Julie's, marriage. I pulled out the DVD, put it into the player and "voila," I was instantly transported back to 1993 and our first big family wedding. The one Julie and I planned. As the DVD played, I was surprised at myself, how full of light, laughter and fun I was. I tend to think back to those years after the trial as dark healing years, but that impression is just wrong. I sometimes forget that I have an uncanny ability to compartmentalize. The DVD proves it. Clearly I had not missed any of the fun or the excitement of our only daughter's special occasion; even though it was during the aftermath of the trial and in the midst of the publicity for my book, *Cry the Darkness.* The video is proof. It shows that I was in no way wallowing in despair over my father or the ugliness of the recent events. However, I do recall that I was still suffering awful nightmares, but none of that was visible on the video.

Our family has an ability to be flexible. Planning a big wedding, 325 were coming to our back yard for the reception, could lead to stress for many families. If we had stress it was in a good way. Of course I am not guaranteeing that the end result would have made it into *Modern Bride* magazine. It could be that we had an odd combination of elements, but we were all happy with it, and our friends and family were too polite to ever say anything negative. As mother-of-the bride, my strong-suit was fully mobilized. Those who know me well, know I am the queen of inclusiveness. That strategy meant that "all ideas" were welcome. Whatever idea any one had was included, clever or not. Julie wanted baskets full of candy kisses on the tables. No problem. Ken and Justin liked the idea of big cowboy hats and boots for the groom's party. No problem. Ken wanted a big western barbecue. I needed a catering company to oversee the cake, champagne toasts, and the non-barbecue part of the food. Another of us liked the idea of a flutist playing Andes music while the guests arrived at the reception. I can still hear Julie's excited voice, "How about twinkle lights all over the back yard and we can float flowers in the pool, and I would love a harpist at the church as the guests gather!" Then Ken chimed in with the idea of a potato bar. Julie wanted fresh flowers in the porta potties. We included all of it!

My age-mate girl friends were also planning their daughters' weddings. They shared stories of bickering and lost tempers. One of my girl friends told me that her daughter-bride had stopped talking to her! Another eloped. Julie and I just smiled and sailed through it. Choosing the wedding gown and bridesmaids' dresses went the same way; she tried many on. Picked one. Modeled it for me at the bridal store. I cried over how beautiful she was. She bought it and that was that! We were relaxed. I knew that the most important thing would be for Julie to be happy. If she were happy, then I was happy. I did smile a bit to myself every time her bridesmaid Teri whined, "I want to be Julie. I want to live Julie's life!" I took that as a compliment. I think our strategy worked.

The DVD reminded me how much I had kept the video rolling during the days before the wedding. Armed with my trusty professional quality video recorder, I would record anyone who came in my path, including the poor substitute UPS man. The footage of me rushing out the front door, camera mounted on my shoulder, tells it all. I informed this unsuspecting young driver that we were getting ready for a wedding.

"Hi. You're new aren't you? These are wedding gifts. It's in just a few days. I'm making a pre-event documentary. Do you wanna be part of it?" I enthused as I warmed up my camera. He smiled at me as I filmed him and seemed interested; a deer-in-the-headlights kind of interest. As the video continued to play, it showed that the next day I was again armed with that camera and this time I caught our regular driver. The tape shows our conversation.

"Hey we missed you yesterday. Someone else brought the boxes!"

"Hi there, news travels fast. I already heard all about the nutty lady up the street with the rogue video camera," he replied laughing. "That substitute entertained all the drivers while we loaded up this morning. Your interview was the hot story on our route yesterday!"

"That's me, providing a bit of comedic relief!" I said as I grinned to him and accepted the packages.

The film showed that our regular driver quickly lost the spotlight of my camera as two huge Party City delivery trucks came to the front of the house. I'm certain I was thinking "new prey" for my "movie." Immediately another big truck, this one with four porta-potties strapped to its flatbed, rolled in front of our house. I was delighted as more and more people came around, I was ready for them: Julie's friends, the bridal party, my sister, the neighbors, they were all fair game for my movie extravaganza. Dan was grading the vacant acre next to our property for the parking lot. I couldn't get him to stop work for some facetime with my machine. He did however 'wave" the grader on the back of the giant yellow skip loader for me. He somehow bounced the rear basket up and down as if to say "hello." Funny!

So our house became "Control Central" for this elaborate team of pre-wedding people. There was the troop of women caterers plus the town's historical society working on barbecuing their famous Santa Maria tri-tip. Tony, our friend and president of the historical society, had surprised us with the offer that for a donation to the society, he and his crew would set up their equipment under a tent and grill a meal that we would never forget. They did and it was fantastic.

On this particular spring afternoon of reminiscing with the video, I was resting after a hot and gallopy two-hour horseback ride with Ken and our oldest grand daughter, Jill. I was enjoying this side trip down wedding memory lane. About 20 minutes into it, Ken came in from the yard and I shared some details that we had forgotten. Ken sat down and we continued to watch, each of us lost in the sweetness of those busy crazy days leading up to the wedding.

"Donna, do you remember that the bar we set up was sinking into the ground? It was over the septic tank and it was sinking!" Ken was chuckling as he recalled, "I very calmly got someone to lift up the other end of the it and we walked nonchalantly across the yard to a dry spot. Boy what a mess if a guest had sunk their heels into the mud from the septic system! It would not have been the effect we were after!"

There was a lot of footage of Dan working. He was hammering wood for a stage or he was nailing plywood sheeting for the dance floor. The playback of memories was still rolling when Ken got up and left, midway. I thought it odd, as the film was captivating, seeing all of us as we were nearly 20 years ago, but I settled back to my viewing. Later Ken told me that he could not take watching it. He went to water the flowers and to shed tears.

"Honey, why?" I asked. "It was so great! We were all having so much fun. You should have seen the ending. The next day, if you remember, I just happened to catch Julie rollerblading around the dance floor before it was taken down. She was so cute. After all that excitement of her lovely self as the elegant bride, contrasted with the "kid" in her racing around the dance floor on her skates yelling, 'Mom I don't know how to rollerblade' and off she would go! My voice-over was, 'Ladies and gentlemen, this is the first public debut of the new Mrs. Bell!'"

Ken paused for a minute and then remarked, "It was too much. It made me realize what an amazing life we have had and it makes me so sad to think there're not that many more years to go. Donna, it has been such a blessing, the way our family has lived. It just makes me sad that we have been so happy."

I knew what Ken meant. Our lives had been party to the horrible, miserable and the awful, (how many families are forced to take such drastic action against a father?), but the wonderful and magnificent have far outweighed the ugly. I thought back some more to that wedding week. It was August 1993 and our beautiful twenty-five year-old daughter Julina was marrying wonderful 6'3" tall Justin Bell. He was a great guy and we were all happy about the match. I was excited to bring his height gene into our shorter DNA pool!

On the day of the wedding itself, it was wild at our house. While I was pressing Julie's long gown, all the bridesmaids were in and out. Everyone seemed to have a job. I remember that while I was ironing I turned around and looked out the window to see the bridal party lined up practicing their Macarana exhibition dance on the new floor. That was delicious fun to watch. They were acting like the teens they were not so long ago, and then to top it off, I saw them all jump into the pool!

In the middle of all this my mom came over to deliver her wedding gift in person, she took one look at all of Julie's NCAA championship soccer trophies sitting on a shelf with the wedding veil draped over them. That put her over the edge and she burst into tears. Actually, we were all pretty fragile that way during those pre-vows days. It was a life-turning point to have Julie marry. We knew nothing would ever be quite the same again. It was a mix of feelings. The rehearsal dinner was also a tear-jerker with Julie sharing what each of the seven bridesmaids had meant to her across her life. Next, Justin, who is typically more reserved, stood up and told us the moment when he knew that he had met the "girl of his dreams."

And that was just the warm-up to the actual church wedding. The feminist in me could not "give my daughter away" so we compromised. As the harpist stopped playing, and the chords to "Here Comes the Bride" bellowed out from the organ, Ken, serious-faced, with his exquisite daughter at his side, began the slow walk down the aisle. They entered the sanctuary from a side door, and when they arrived at the front entrance, I joined them, and together the three of us walked Julie, our lovely, athletic, delightful, funny girl, into her new life where we "presented" her to be married. It was a time dividing milestone.

The reception lasted for hours; dancing, toasting, eating and laughing. During my remarks, I reminded Julie that as a little girl she dreamed of getting married in our back yard. Her fantasies had come true. I think all of our fantasies had come true. The last crowning piece of the event was that Rick surprised everyone earlier that week by announcing his engagement to Jenny, the vivacious young lady he had been dating from his law firm. It was a time for celebration and we reveled in every minute of it.

Julie and Justin returned from their honeymoon and life got back to normal. School started in September and we resumed our regular lives, except more excitement was brewing in the Rick and Jenny world as their spring wedding plans and activities kicked into high gear.

Before long there were more bridal showers and luncheons. Jen found the dress of her fantasies and bought it well before Rick proposed which gave us all something to tease her about! On a warm spring evening, Ken and I hosted an intimate rehearsal dinner at our home and enjoyed getting to know Jenny's family. One of the highlights of that night for me was observing this future daughter-in-law with her two young nieces. I can still see her bending down on the grass next to the red-headed four year-old. Jenny delicately picked a fluff ball from the grass. With reverence, she whispered something to the child and then with some fanfare they blew that fuzzy dandelion head together. I captured that vision in my memory (for once I was without my video camera!) It gave me a glimpse into the kind of mother she would be for my future grandchildren.

Their plans culminated in a traditional church wedding in Corona Del Mar. One of the most awe inspiring aspects of that ceremony was the sublime duet sung by our son-in-law, Justin's parents. As accomplished singers, they held us spellbound with their resonating tones and the reverent manner in which they sang to each other about love. They were beyond sensational, a perfect segue into the exchange of vows during which both Rick and Jenny were poised and relaxed. Jenny rented out Cano's waterfront restaurant in Newport Beach for the dinner and dancing reception. Julie tied cans to their car so that the happy couple was forced to leave under cover of lots of clanging noise! It was a memorable and beautiful event.

A few weeks later, Ken and I were enjoying Mother's Day brunch with Julie and Justin on the patio of a San Diego restaurant when they surprised us with big news! The first grandchild would be coming in early January 1995. Ken and I were elated! In the following months, I could think of little else. I remember that I was training volunteer staff members at Laura's House, a women's shelter, one weekend and I was giving the participants a week by week count-down until I became a grandmother! Clearly, I had gotten a bit off subject!

So if we thought there'd been a lot of bridal showers with those two weddings, there were more parties to come; the cycle of baby showers began! Julie has always had a lot of friends. Everyone wanted to host a shower for her. It was a festive time, but life does not always offer us the easiest road. In the midst of all this bliss, the reality of how harsh life can be raised its ugly head again.

Julie and her best friend Angela had dreamed of having their families together. They really wanted to raise their kids side by side. It was not a passing thought. I remember that Angela gave Julie a framed painting of a little brunette child walking hand in hand with a little blonde child, representing their future children. This was something they had dreamed about and had actually managed to make happen. Both women were expecting their first-borns around the same date so clearly a joint baby party was in order. All of us, family members and friends, were thrilled for the girls as we planned this big dual shower. A few days before the party an unforeseen circumstance played out.

A doctor's visit showed that Angela's 27-week pregnancy was in jeopardy. Serious complications were found. In order to save the baby, the delivery had to be induced immediately, *that day*, even though it was way too early. Everyone was devastated, no one more so than the young parents and her parents, for she was an only child. This was 1994 and the survival rate for a preemie was not great. We were all at the hospital. I remember standing in the hall when Angela's mother came out from the delivery room. We just held each other for a long time. Finally she whispered, "The baby is here. It's a girl and she is tiny, so tiny. One pound 13 ounces. She is so tiny and beautiful. All we can do now is pray." With that each of us choked out a sob. None of us had experience with anything like this.

For weeks and weeks the baby stayed in the hospital in an incubator. When she was finally big enough to ho home there was relief, prayers had been answered. This ordeal was a sobering reminder that life is not always so easy. It was a big lesson for these young people, for all of us. None of us had been sure that the little girl would pull through. But she did. As I write this, I marvel at the incredible young woman she has become. It is her last year of high school. She is perfect in all ways, a top student headed to the University of California at Berkeley, lovely and good-hearted. A miracle.

That scary time was in November of 1994 and a short time later Julie, too, had complications resulting from her pregnancy. She suffered toxemia and was put on mandatory bed rest, missing out on Thanksgiving gatherings as she worried about her unborn baby and how she would complete her master's degree. There was one last paper that had to be written and turned in. She wanted this completed before the baby arrived, but she had to lie down, all the time. Since she could not type lying down, we got the idea that she would dictate her final paper to me from her place on the floor. That sounds easy, but at the time I only knew WordPerfect as a word processing program, not Word which she used. It seems funny now, but I it wasn't then. Every time Julie had to make a change in her important last paper, I had a struggle trying to process it, but somehow we made it work and graduation was assured.

Christmas was just days away when a doctor visit revealed that Julie's toxemia was getting worse, the baby was in danger. The birth had to be moved up by three weeks. This would not be a January baby. The delivery had to be induced. Quickly. It was three days before Christmas when we all arrived at Tri-Cities Hospital.

Ken and I happened to park our car next to Julie and Justin's in the hospital lot. As we walked past it I spotted the baby carrier set up in the back seat. Suddenly it all became so real to me. I choked back tears. Anything could go wrong. The tears spilled down my cheeks. I prayed that soon our little grandson would be strapped into that carrier.

We joined Julie in her room. The pitocin had already been administered to begin the labor. As the labor continued, its intensity heightened. I could see that the delivery nurse was becoming increasingly more anxious. She conferred with the doctor over the telephone. We knew why. We could all see the digital monitor's report which showed both the mother and the baby's blood pressure. The various medications given to help Julie's high blood pressure were adversely affecting the baby's heart rate. We could see with each beat that his tiny heart was beating more and more slowly. We had been told that the normal range was around 120 beats per minute. We were warned that only as long so the rate remained above 100, would the baby be safe.

The time seemed to pass in slow motion. Our vigil became increasingly more silent as our anxiety levels escalated. Gathered around her bed, Julie clutched my hand with her right hand and her husband's with her left. We watched the steady fall of the baby's heart rate. One hundred and ten, one hundred, ninety-eight, one hundred, ninety-eight, ninety-seven. In the silence we saw the nurse's face change. It was a mask of urgency. Abruptly she left the room. We knew this was serious. Ninety. My mouth felt dry, my heart pounded. Horrible thoughts of possibly losing my daughter and my baby grandchild screamed in my thoughts. It was agonizing. Time seemed to stand still.

I looked away from the baby's blood pressure readings. My stomach was in knots. Julie tightened her grip. I held on. The nurse came in again and checked the digital monitor. Her worried expression remained carved into her face.

From the metal hospital bed Julie continued to clutch both my hand and Justin's. Ninety two. Ninety. Ken stood nearby. A sentry. I felt rigid with anxiety.

After what seemed an eternity but was probably much shorter, the young doctor burst into the room. The space became a whirl wind of action as he pulled the delivery lights down from above the hospital bed. He hissed out some worried orders to the nurse. Suddenly Julie's contractions increased dramatically and the doctor yelled out, "Push now!" A hush had engulfed the room. The scene played out in slow motion.

Ten minutes later we stood awed by the sight of this new little boy. He was blue in color, thin, but strong looking. I watched as he slowly opened his eyes to the world for the very first time. He seemed to focus on me through very large luminous eyes. I choked as I held his gaze. *I know that baby! Goodness, big eyes, big, like Julie had when she was born!"* I gasped for air.

As I steadied myself and took in oxygen, a memory came to me of a very similar baby I had held 26 years before. He reminded me of newborn Julie. The doctor massaged his tiny back to get him to take his first breath, immediately we heard his lusty cry. Relief flooded us. Tears filled my eyes and my stomach did a quick somersault. *How could this be, this miracle of life.* I did not even try to talk. I knew I couldn't. What a jumble of emotions: joy, relief, excitement, pride, astonishment that I was part of this incredible chain of human life. I felt my link with the force that is life.

I smiled a wet-faced smile to my daughter. She and her husband embraced silently. None of us said a word, we couldn't! I looked at Ken and he held my eyes for a long time as it to say, "We made it. All our dreams did come true. This is what it means to be a family."

After a while some of us found our voices. There were hugs and more tears as little baby Jake was foot-printed and weighed and kept warm. That experience highlighted for me the importance of our human connections and of our commitments to one another. I felt part of something important and I still do. These loved ones bind me to something bigger than I am. Something higher.

The next day Julie and the baby were allowed to go home. Because we had all been with Julie in the days before Christmas, she and Justin, exhausted with the new arrival, had decided to stay home in San Diego for Christmas day. But that morning hearing the tears in Julie's voice, as she was clearly missing her whole big family on Christmas day, we piled into the car.

Rick, Jenny, Dan, Ken and I, loaded all of our gifts and food and sped down the freeway to San Diego to bring Christmas to Julie. When we surprised her an hour or so later she was speechless. More tears, but happy ones. It had been a rough go for her, but she found strength and comfort in the love and support of her family.

THE POPULATION EXPLOSION CONTINUES

When baby Jake was three-months-old, Julie and I decided that he was big enough for professional photos. At the photo studio we had propped him up next to a big soft yellow alphabet block when suddenly my cell phone rang.

"Hello?"

"Donna, Hi. I am glad you picked up. My water just broke. The baby's coming. I am rushing off to the hospital now."

"Oh my gosh. Jenny. I am in San Diego. I am coming right now. I will be at the hospital soon. I will get more film!"

Overcome with excitement Julie and I shortened the photo session and I made a dash for the freeway to get back up to Orange County before Rick and Jenny's baby came into the world. I drove straight to the hospital stopping only to get more containers of film, as I had been assigned the job of photographing this event. About 10 hours later, at three in the morning, Jenny delivered a beautiful little blonde girl whom they named Jillian. I could not believe how lucky I was, now I had Jake and Jill!

Two years later both Julie and Jenny presented little baby sisters to their first-borns. As the years passed and Ken and I felt that we had hit the grandparent jackpot. We all joined together for family Mammoth Mountain ski trips, enjoyed crowded weekends at our mountain cabin and continued our family tradition of Catalina days. Life was full and lots of fun.

By 1998 our family was growing so fast that we had already out grown our little one bedroom mountain cabin near Big Bear. Years earlier we had purchased a 1/12th interest in an old fishing camp that was situated on the Santa Ana River. It included apple orchards, streams and 120 acres of open space. We all loved it but with all the gestating and lactating that was going on, the moms took priority using the one good bedroom in the cabin. Ken and I were relegated to sleeping in the moldy sleephouse across the lawn.

The sleephouse boasted an original 1900's chamber pot, which might sound charming, but the reality of using it, was not so glamorous. Ken soon became allergic to the sleephouse's mildewy dampness and this was clearly not my idea of how to spend vacation days. We decided we had to add on to the cabin. We planned to build a big great room that would join the two old river rock structures and accommodate our family.

As a new master builder, Dan headed up the project, enjoying a chance to practice his design-building skills. He had already had the foundation trenches built when we were all at the cabin for my dear friend Janet's daughter's big tent wedding on the lawn. We were all excited about this big event. On this particular Saturday morning I was standing in the kitchen looking out at the foundation forms with 4-year-old Jake standing next to me. As Jake examined the construction site, he called out to his dad, grandpa, and uncles, "Come on guys, let's build it!" And we did. That memory is one of my little treasures. Little Jakey wanted to get cracking with the hammer and nails right now! Ten years later he would begin spending his summers working for Ken's construction company, and after that to engineering school.

The mountain cabin not only allowed us an escape from city life but it also brought us a group of close friends. I will share more about this important slice of our family life a bit later.

FIGHTING INTERNAL DEMONS

It would be a mistake to think that Ken and I and our children got past that horrific 15 month long trial against my father and that somehow life miraculously settled down to cabin additions and lots of beautiful babies. It was not like that. Probably the most difficult decision in my entire life was to come clean with my dark secret to Ken. Imagine that 25 years into a marriage your husband has to finally learn that "oh by the way honey I forgot to mention that during my entire childhood I fought to stay on track and happy and sane when in the dark recesses of my psyche I had to constantly push back the devastation of being continually raped since I was nine years-old by the very daddy who helped me with my home work, made sure I had a party dress and who threatened to kill me if I "*talked.*"

I promise that my secret would have gone to my grave with me had it not been for the fact that I learned my little niece Keely was being babysat by dad everyday, where she was alone in the house with him for hours at a time. If not for this discovery, these words would not be on the page, nor would anyone know my truth. When my little niece's mom and adult sister came to my home and shared with me about what dad was doing to Keely, I could no longer hide behind my years of built-up denial: denial that I used to convince myself that dad was old and infirm and that he would not bother the many children in the family; a form of denial that was weakening by the months as my father's behavior was reported to me. My mind could no longer hide out. I was struck by acute post traumatic stress disorder. I had panic attacks and nightmares. I had to get help. I knew I had to stop him but I was too conditioned by fear to act. I decided to get therapeutic support not only for my own well being, but to develop enough strength and a strategy to stop him. I went to weekly sessions for several months, and then I knew that I had to take action and that I *had* to tell my husband.

Growing up in the 1950's in the culture of *The Ozzie and Harriet* and the *Leave it to Beaver* shows where moms were stay-at-homes, and wanting more than anything to keep my marriage together, I followed the model of traditional wife and mother at home, while I was a career woman on the outside. I made dinner every night, cleaned up the kitchen, did the shopping and ran the home. I still do. I actually like it. The women I knew were *not* having children and raising them while holding down a full time job. Most either stayed at home raising their children or they were career gals sans children. Part of me felt guilty for being out of the home, even though we certainly needed the funds I earned. My best role model for having a beautiful marriage was Leanne's mom, and she was compliant toward her dominant husband. It was what I knew.

Through therapy, I began to understand how much I was allowing myself to be dominated by my husband. And so during those wedding bell and baby shower years, I was working very hard on the internal Donna, and it was not easy. One of my survival strategies as a child was to not make waves. The times when I challenged my father on matters such as telling him that keeping up my A average in high school, running the remnants of our grandfather's pharmacy after school, and building a house on the weekends was too much. I was exhausted and suffered chronic tonsillitis. My protests fell on deaf ears and in fact were met with harsh consequences. I learned that to stand up to daddy was to lose. To lose Big! My survival technique became one of shutting up and putting up. I brought that technique to my marriage.

All in all I underwent three years of intense therapy, plus my own studies throughout my doctoral program which focused on perpetrators and their victims. One of the great salvations across my life has been the cognitive process. If my mind could grasp information, I could steer my feelings in a better direction. Through therapy I grew stronger. In addition I began writing out the awful truth into the pages of *Cry the Darkness*. The more I wrote, the more free I felt. I was letting go of some of the horror.

I began to see that my modus operandi of accommodation was not always working that well for me. I came to understand that I could no longer tolerate Ken's controlling tendencies nor would I allow myself to be put on the back burner of his activities. I would tell him, "Kenny I am not even on your dance card." He would look at me and sometimes listen, but the old ways continued.

Ken's survival strategy growing up in his chaotic alcoholic home was to be anywhere but home. He brought that behavior into our marriage. He was busy coaching football and wrestling, working full time as a high school administrator, teaching college night classes, and serving on the city council and being mayor. He was not around much, and I said little. Very little!

In fairness to him, I admit that I allowed negative behavior. I had not fussed much when he had angry blow-ups about money. When my handsome husband had emotional outbursts, I just sucked it up. It was not good, but growing up I was used to emotional tantrums from my father. With counseling, change was in the air.

As I grew stronger I demanded more equality in our marriage. Ken confesses to me now that it was very frightening for him to have me begin to stand up for myself. I have recently learned from the new studies on cognitive neuroscience that our brains hold deeply imbedded neural maps that can keep us locked in old behaviors. It is possible to change them, but it requires mindfulness to do so and I was becoming mindful.

The more I studied about codependency and the more I taught my interpersonal relationship students positive tools for change, I began to see that my own behaviors had to be altered. I had allowed this.

When one begins to change, the entire web of their interpersonal relationships is affected. It can lead to a rocky road. Ken either had to change or we could not go forward as a couple. To his great credit he got into therapy and began to deal with his own anxiety issues. He learned that he suffered from "free floating anxiety," a residue from the parental fighting and drunkenness he experienced at home during his childhood. Ken learned tools to help with his own depressive tendencies. We began to talk about some of the real issues we had between us, and slowly things improved. He still falls back into controlling ways and will still try to micromanage me, but I use the tools I have learned about reframing an event. I can see the bigger picture. I have a very devoted husband who is the great love of my life. Is he easy? Not at all. Do I love him more than life? Yes I do. Is it simple to maintain a forty-eight year long marriage? No, but the rewards for hanging in there have been far greater than some anger storms or criticism about spending a few cents more at the wrong gas station.

When Ken walks in the door at night, after he kisses me hello, he will always be caught saying, "let me get out of these clothes and into something more comfortable, I want to hear all about your day." And he really does. He cares about my students, my clients, my organizations, and everything about the kids. He is my true love.

Before we leave the topic of the traditional submissive wife, I think it is important to understand human behavior within the context of the times.

I was married in 1964 as historic shifts shook the status quo of the free world. During my senior year of college Betty Friedan's *Feminine Mystique* was released foreshadowing a seismic cultural paradigm shift in women's attitudes toward staying-at-home.

Armed with the new birth control pill and the power of the human rights marches vibrating across the social landscape, change was coming. But it did not happen fast. Some of the women of my generation were gently knocking at the glass ceiling at work, while others continued to embrace the traditional model. Still others were questioning their role at home.

I recall that as a young 27 year old faculty member at my college in 1970 there was a welcome tea for faculty and staff hosted during the first week of school by the Faculty Wives Association. The ladies were dressed in white gloves and wore large hats. It was a nice affair with a lovely buffet table set with petit fours. I was engaged in a conversation when one of the wives came up to me and said, "Dear, this section is only for faculty. The secretarial staff seats are over there." The male colleague I had been chatting with turned to her and explained that I was a tenured faculty member. As the woman took in this new reality she turned red and stalked away! She was speechless. Her worldview did not allow for this young blonde woman to be a teacher!

During that same year, Ken and I chose to add a third child to our family. As the spring semester wore on, my girth began to show. It was not acceptable for a faculty member to teach while pregnant, but the 60's influence resonated silently in the background. The result was that no one actually acknowledged my pregnancy.

One day I had a meeting with the chancellor of the college district. He too ignored my billowing midsection. He only looked at my eyes. There were no baby showers and no announcements about Donna's baby's birth in the faculty bulletin. It was an early version of "don't ask, don't tell."

However, one contingent of social activists at my college did seem to notice. They were adamant supporters of Paul Erlich and his *Population Bomb*. In their enthusiasm to stop the world's population growth, they took to wrapping his books in black paper and sending them to the maternity wards at local hospitals. A kind of macabre warning, I guess. That was a terrible time for me. As a result of looks and not so subtle comments, I felt personally persecuted in the faculty lounge. I had to stop going in at all.

In subsequent years I continued to feel a chill of disgust from those colleagues because of my third child. And so as I tell about the early dynamic between my husband and myself, you have to understand the social climate at the time. It might be hard to believe now, but even though I was a high-wage earner, I was not allowed to have a credit card in my own name because I was a married woman.

Gloria Steinem writes about being turned away from the lobby of the Plaza Hotel in New York City by the doorman because she was a single woman! She also reported that women were not allowed to eat lunch at the Oak Room in that hotel lest their chatting distract the businessmen at lunch!

Societal rules are powerful influences. It almost seems funny now to think that women were not allowed to lunch in a public hotel or that a college professor could not have her own credit card, or a third child.

Happily, times have changed and I will always be grateful that my husband changed along with them and with me. Even more important to me is the fact that there are two generations of women following me who have the freedom to choose to stay-at-home or to have a career with children. In fact it is illegal for an employer to even ask about marriage or children. The cultural changes are reflected not just in the fact that maternity leave now exists, but today there is recognition of the father's role and there is family leave. School districts routinely allow for shared teaching contracts so moms have a more flexible schedule during the baby years. Corporate America has on-site child care centers. A new era is in place but it was not without sacrifice for some of us who felt like we were on the firing line during the 60's and 70's.

CHAPTER TWO: AFTERMATH OF THE BATTLE - ACTIVISM

"All that is necessary for evil to triumph is for good men to do nothing."
Edmund Burke

May 20, 2012
San Juan Capistrano, CA

This morning I took two of my Golden Retrievers, Tessie and Zoe, out for one of our regular four mile walks. I had left my IPod behind and was more highly attuned to my environment than usual. We ventured into the dogs' favorite place; the creek bed. They love to sniff around in the overgrown plants and to splash in the water. I managed a dry crossing, relying on some big rocks, and climbed up onto the dike to the walking trail.

As the dogs and I marched along we came to a quarter horse gazing at us silently from behind her wooden corral. I could not help myself. I approached her, slowly, with my hand held out for her to smell. She inhaled; I stepped closer. She inhaled again and I touched the soft velvet of her nose. She leaned further out from her enclosure. I petted her head. She pushed herself more fully into me, nudging for more attention.

I stroked her massive head as I studied the veins concealed beneath her shiny hide. She had long eyelashes. She leaned in even more. I could not help but puzzle what brings humans and animals together like this? What is this connection? As a warmth swept through me, I thought about what my clients were always saying: how I see the positive in things. Why? I do not know, but my soul is nourished by the simplest of things: the velvet of the horse's muzzle, the yellow on the flitting wings of the nearby butterflies, the sight of Tessie, fast asleep, lying on her back with all four legs sticking straight up into the air!

I revel in these little things. The other night. Ken and I were invited to one of our granddaughter's school performances. I was on two year old Gracie duty while our son Dan ran the video camera on our performer, Eleven year old Lauren and kept track of eight year old Allison. Ken was running late. The auditorium lights dimmed, the audience hushed, and for about fifteen minutes, Gracie held it together. Soon she caught my attention and patting the empty seat between us whispered, "Poppa?"

"He will be coming along soon. Let's watch your sister."

A few more minutes passed, this time with more urgency, "Poppa?"

Boredom was setting in. She climbed off her chair and explored my purse. An old mint. Ah, that kept her quiet for awhile. "Poppa?"

This time I tried the string cheese. That worked for a few more minutes. Finally, Ken quietly slid into the seat next to me. Gracie immediately spotted him and made a beeline for his lap. With a strong well muscled arm, my husband of 48 years scooped up the little girl.

In that moment of greeting I took in a world of information. She is to be our last grand baby and I cannot help but mentally record every detail. I noted her lowered eye lids and then how she quickly opened them. At two she was batting her eyes!! Then ever so slowly she delivered a huge smile and then instantly looked away! I was laughing inside. *Miss Coy! We gals learn our tricks early!* The gesture seemed instinctive and thoroughly feminine. In fact, I am still laughing out loud just thinking of it! She is such her Poppa's Girl!

As I recalled these thoughts, that familiar sweet feeling flowed through me, no doubt oxytocin or dopamine set loose in my blood stream. The sweetness of the moment, of falling in love with my husband all over again, filled me. I sat back in my chair and relaxed. This was not something new. I had experienced this before. Each time I witness that magic between my husband and one of our many grandchildren, my heart skips a bit.

Perhaps the chaos of my childhood gave me this ability, I don't know; but somehow I have learned to see ordinary moments in a kind of Technicolor, even something as simple as Ken lifting up our little girl and the flash of her smile. I feel gratitude, not just for the beauty of family life, but for being able to pause and see it, to feel it, and to immerse myself in it.

As I continued to stroke the muzzle of the bay horse I thought about how I have learned to nurture myself; a very good thing. I remembered when I was about twelve and wanted to walk into the ocean and never come back. Dark thoughts. Somehow I have figured out how to take care of myself. One of the best pieces of advice my grandmother ever gave me was, "Donna no one can take care of you but yourself." I took that to heart and I do a good job of it.

During the years of raising my own children, I understood that the elaborate birthday parties I hosted for them were also for me. I tried to raise them the way I might have wished to have been raised. That was something that Ken and I consciously committed to from the beginning. We also gave them lots of room. We tried to leave them to their own devices unless it was dangerous. We let them be.

My mind scanned across the past twenty years, since the release of my book, *Cry the Darkness*. When listeners in my audiences would ask me, "Why are you so happy?" I shared this with you earlier, but I did not mention that sometimes I would read a subtext, "Donna, what is WRONG with you that you seem so right? "What choices have you made that have allowed you to be this woman we see?" Early on I was at a loss for an explanation. I knew it was not just luck. I get that for each of us "luck" is about our everyday choices; our daily actions.

I thought about my grown children; their weddings, the births of the eleven grandchildren; my students, my rich teaching career, the love of my husband, my fancy new titanium hip, the six books I have authored, appearing on Oprah's show and the back stage metal detectors, of my trek through the Himalayas last September and bathing that 11,000 pound elephant in the Yeti River, finding our brother who had been given up at birth, the list would be long. What has allowed me to thrive? How have I kept my head out of the muck? Recalling a line from *Cry the Darkness*, "By age nine, I was an opera stage extra, an auto mechanic, and a *real* woman." Was that it? Or was it that by age fifteen, my sister and I ran the remnants of our grandfather's pharmacy as a sundry store after school and on weekends while we completed our homework in the back room, and after hours, helped build a house, sometimes working all night long on plumbing to pass a morning inspection. Was it the hard work or was it the drive to become independent so that I would no longer be at the mercy of someone stronger and more powerful?

As I resumed my walk along the path the dogs raced ahead. I continued my thoughts. I have always been hungry to figure out the secrets of the human experience. I vividly remember sitting on the floor of my grandfather's drug store in the book section, surrounded by comic books and magazines, studying a new book that had come out on psychosomatic illnesses. I know that I was younger than nine years old because our family had not yet moved away from the beach. As I read, a new world opened up to me. Of course I had to look up what "psychosomatic" meant, but that book taught me there is a mind-body connection; that some illnesses may be rooted in the internal workings in our minds. That was big news to me. I thought about my father's bleeding ulcers and his constant conflict with the world. I suspect that those early writings whetted my appetite for more ideas, more science, to unlock the mysteries of what makes us humans tick.

Anyway, this is one of my weird little secrets; digesting such thoughts, picking at the scab of the human condition. Some might think it odd, but I enjoy stopping the moving picture of my life in mid frame and mulling it over. I don't know if others do that because it is not actually the kind of thing that one shares, "Uh, do you stop in the middle of the significant moments in your life and reflect on what they mean?" Probably it is safer to keep quiet about such things. Empowerment means knowing when and with whom to share such things.

I don't know what others do, and would be embarrassed to ask. I secretly wonder if I have taken Socrates too much to heart when he proclaimed that "an unexamined life is a life not worth living." Clearly, I have had plenty of time to examine mine. Maybe that is another gift of getting to live so long. I remember the last day of my undergraduate college life. Graduation from USC had taken place, and I sat on my roommates' stripped bed as she had already moved out. I leaned against the open second story window of the sorority house and looked out on 28th street, ("The Row,") and carefully documented that this day was a turning point in my life. I knew my life would never be the same. I noticed the cars parked along the curb, the fresh-faced students up and down the street, moving boxes out to their cars. I admired the trim lawns and flowering gardens. I did not feel sad, but I was carefully sorting and filing the memories of those two blissful years of being free of my father and living in the Alpha Gam house. I was to bid The Lavender Room goodbye in a few moments and paused to immortalize it, for even then, June 16, 1964, I knew that the two years at USC and in that sorority house had been the powerful steps into my future life, the life of *my choosing*.

***

Twenty seven years later, another life framing moment took place. It occurred on a Sunday Morning, August 4, 1991, to be exact. After breakfast at our condo in Mammoth, California, Ken had finally broached the subject that sat like an uninvited elephant in the room.

37

"Donna, I think the *Los Angeles Times* has arrived at Pioneer Market by now. I'll go get those copies. It's time to see it in print." This was to be the day my soul would be laid bare with the cover story of the Sunday edition of the *Los Angeles Times Magazine*.

My heart squeezed more tightly as I wiped off the kitchen counters from breakfast. "Uh, I guess so. There's nothing to be gained by waiting." I replied. I remember that I kept averting my eyes as I wiped the same spot on the counter, "Kenny you know my life will never be exactly the same after today don't you?"

"Lover, you had to do this. If we had not trusted the story to Lynn Smith of the *Times* there's no telling what kind of field day the press might have had with it! What if some eager reporter had believed your dad's story; believed that you were trying to frame him so you could get Keely and his money away from him?"

Ken looked at me. "It will be okay. You have already proven you are one tough cookie! I'll be right back."

I blasted a last half cup of coffee in the microwave oven and walked over to my favorite spot, the window seat Ken had built for me. I stared across the valley and studied far away Lake Crowley. It was a familiar and peaceful scene, but there was anything but peace as my insides roiled into an anxious knot.

As I sat curled on the window seat, the familiar fears played across the movie screen of my mind. Everyone at work would soon know about my childhood. Could I lose my wonderful teaching career? Would they fire me? One part of me understood that such an idea was absurd, but another part of me was terrified. What about Ken's career in local politics? Would he now be ridiculed? We would be the subject of gossip and whispers. What about our children? Could they keep their heads up while people *knew?*

At one point during the investigation into my father's case, the detective, Jim Bowen, in charge of sex crimes, confided to Ken and me that in his 20 years of police work, he had never encountered such an insidious case of sexual abuse across so many generations by one perpetrator as this case. He had said, "I have never heard anything like this before. Seriously Donna, you should write your story."

Leaving the detective's office that afternoon, driving south to Orange County, Ken had said the same thing, that I should write my story. I put up a strong resistance. All the reasons why I could not: too hard; don't know how. The discussion continued on the long ride home with me finally conceding that perhaps I could find a ghost writer.

A few months later, while Ken was away gathering our oldest son up from law school in San Francisco, I had begun the tentative strokes of the keys on the computer. Before the end of the summer I had poured 600 pages of my heart out onto the paper. I had done it. I felt better for having my truth inside the computer, as my magical thinking had it, but this magazine story would be read by thousands of people. No one had seen my book, yet!

From the safety of the window seat I continued to examine my emotions. I knew that my fears had intensified during the last few days, since the *Times* reporter, Lynn, had called to tell us that the editors of the *Los Angeles Times Magazine* had decided that it would be the cover story, big picture and all. It was horrifying. I could barely sleep more than a few hours at a time.

Ken returned with the papers, and true to what we had been told, there it was, a big cover story featuring a black and white photo of my handsome young dad sitting on the porch at our beach cottage with his arm around my five-year-old self and my sister Sandy standing nearby. The head line read, *Daddy's Girls: It took the Landis Family 40 years to face its darkest secret.*

I knew that there was going to be no hiding from this. My stomach had knotted over and I had been right, there was no hiding ever again.

With a little shake of my head I forced myself back to the present. I so enjoyed walking with the dogs and for the moment they had disappeared into the creek for a quick dip in the muddy water.

THE MEDIA CALLS

The phone was ringing, ringing, ringing. For weeks after the cover story, Hollywood producers called competing for the film rights to our story. The *Times* bundled up hundreds of letters to the editors meant for us and mailed the bulging manila envelopes to my home. Women and girls all across Southern California were voicing the hope that our story had given them. The message was the same; they no longer felt alone. Dozens of such letters were printed in the subsequent issues of the magazine. For better or worse our story was out there. The chancellor of the local community college district wrote me a personal letter commending me on my bravery, the national morning news shows dragged me and my sister Cee Cee, the mother of the child for whom we were forced to intervene, to their studios. *Inside Edition* TV show brought crews to our home, Montel Williams, Ron Reagan, Jr., Sally Jessy Raphael, The Leeza Show, AM-LA, The Today Show, all invited us to appear on their broadcasts. The list was long and included the print media. Our story appeared in smaller papers across the country. There were magazine features such as that in *Lear's Magazine* and *Changes Magazine* read by thousands more. *Newsweek* interviewed me, the media were hungry to take a bite out of us.

When the Oprah Winfrey Show called, we knew that for our purposes, exposing the devastation and frequency of child sexual abuse, this was the most important opportunity of all. For years, Oprah had waged a tireless fight against this issue. She demanded an exclusive and she would have it. We had to tell the producers of *60 Minutes* that we could not do their show.

So there we were, a half dozen of us, at the Harpo Studios in Chicago. Ken and I, Cee Cee, our brother Chad and his wife, and my mother. The Oprah Winfrey Show estimated a viewership of ten million and true to her ability, she produced a powerful show. In the days leading up to the broadcast of it, the frequent promos warned the viewers: *"Do not miss this one. This is a story like no other you have ever heard."*

On the day of the taping, we assembled in the green room. Soon we were escorted through the metal detectors. We understood why, a few years earlier on a prime time talk show a guest shot and killed another guest. Oprah was not taking any chances of turning her serious-minded show into a circus sideshow. Once through the detector screening, the make-up artist took over. Nervous, I sat quietly while the young woman tried her best to chat away my fears as she applied a heavy foundation to my face. It was not working! I was an adrenaline-filled wreck. I could not even imagine the result of bringing this sordid truth out to such a large audience. Before long we were called to the studio area.

I watched the master at work. Oprah hugged me and seated me next to her. She took my hand. She joked with her live audience, warming them up by showing that she had a "runner," as she called it, in her stocking. She stretched her leg out. Laughing, she showed off the run. We all laughed. She was down-to-earth, putting her audience at ease. Oprah became just a girlfriend sharing intimacies. Everyone calmed down and relaxed. I took a breath. I felt stronger. I was in the hands of a pro. I could trust her as I understood that she was one of the most influential talk show hosts in the world and her agenda was the same as mine, to make women's lives safer. Oprah changed lives. She is a modern day hero. I forced myself to breathe. Soon the cameras were rolling. The camera zoomed in on her face. In a chilling monologue she implored her viewers to stay tuned.

> *It is a story of power and unbelievable perversion in a family where you would least expect it. Five daughters say that they were forced to have sex with daddy all through their childhood, and then two granddaughters. In a recent case that was reported in the <u>Los Angeles Times Magazine</u> it has come out that this man, an aerospace designer, produced and abused all the females in this family.*

Oprah opened with me. She continued to hold my hand as she drew out the details of my first memory, of being on the way to school for the first day, when dad took me to our empty house and molested me. I remembered it vividly because I was so thrilled to get to start school. First grade. I had been so excited, but after the stop by the house it was "just so dark after that."

Following my interview, Oprah talked to my mother, our sister Cee Cee, and our brother Chad. It was an amazing hour long show. In fact, it was so significant that 20 years later, upon Oprah's retirement in 2011, her producers culled it out and screened a clip of me as part of Oprah's grand finale. So once again, clad in my red business suit, there I was telling my story on prime time TV, that we had to stop dad. He could not be allowed to keep molesting 4 year-old Keely.

It had been a bitter 15 month long legal battle; not just the trial which almost resulted in a mistrial, but the whirlwind of media attention, the struggle of actually writing my story, the angst of knowing that a publisher would have the book in bookstores across the country. It was almost too much, but there was a hard core of determination in me and I never thought of stopping.

I know that my psychological healing was helped by the fact that I buried myself in my doctoral research. I learned many intriguing facts. For instance in the 1970's there was a very popular book by Justice and Rita Blair, *The Broken Taboo*, which stated that incest occurs in just one family per million, and in Jewish households, one case per two million. I discovered that such *facts* were so far from the truth that it was laughable. I had always known that I was different. If I believed that statistic, I would not just be different but would be a freak: one case per million. Yikes! No wonder I never told!

My doctoral studies in psychology provided an opportunity to focus on the issue of child sexual abuse. I learned that reliable research by David Finkelor established that incest cases were frequent and common, and that as many as one in three or four little girls is sexually abused. Even Alfred Kinsey in the late 1940's reported that 24% of the women he interviewed had been violated when they were "preadolescents." Of course the way he wrote it was; that 76% of women had **not** been sexually active with an older boy or man in childhood. He never used the word "abuse," and in fact, slanted his literature to make the issue of sex with kids to appear natural. *No wonder Dad admired Kinsey so much!*

That *Oprah Winfrey Show* appearance was in 1991 and for the next ten years I was regularly summoned for media interviews, opinions and appearances. I was one of the experts on the *Sally Jessy Raphael Show.* Around that time the governor of California was Pete Wilson and he was determined to pass legislation that would put teeth into the seriousness of child molestation. With the power of the governor's office, a group of us were able to eliminate the statute of limitations on child sexual abuse, the law that had prohibited most of my siblings from testifying against our father because more than seven years had passed since their abuse. In 1996 Governor Wilson invited me to be at the bill signing when California led the nation in requiring sexual offenders who were on parole to submit to injections of the drug depo pravo in the hopes of stopping their deviant sexual urges. Authoritative research shows extremely high rates of recidivism for sexual offenders. Across the next few years many other states followed California's lead in criminalizing child sexual abuse. The laws regarding what constitutes menace and duress as applied to child rape were strengthened. In 2004 President George W. Bush signed into law a bill we had worked hard to promote: the first national children's rights bill.

In 1993, my book was published in English by Health Communications, Inc. and appeared in stores. This was the same year I completed my doctoral degree. *Cry the Darkness* attracted foreign publishing houses and within a few years was available in seven languages. It was the best selling non-fiction book in the history of the Egmont Publishers in Norway. The publishers flew Ken and me to Norway to promote the book. During the ten days in Norway, I interviewed for television, radio and print media. It was an interesting trip, my first out of the country in two decades. My college roommate Janet coordinated our visit with her Norwegian cousins. They took us sightseeing all over the country. When we were finally leaving Oslo, Janet's cousin picked up the Sunday edition of the Norwegian newspaper. He held it up for us to see, our story covered the entire front page of the paper, top to bottom. I remember that I was shocked that this story was such a big deal in Norway. I knew sexual abuse was a problem in Scandinavia as well as in other countries, but I was surprised at the amount of media attention it was getting, perhaps it was just a big story that helped to sell newspapers. Whatever the agenda, it was clear that predators would have a harder time hiding in their secret corners.

The next year my book came out in Denmark and again I flew to promote it and to spotlight what happens to kids. I vividly recall being the guest speaker in a beautiful 500 year old church. The sanctuary was filled to capacity. I scanned the audience and saw a few hundred devastated faces. My inner being burned with pain at the vision of all those beautiful women who had their innocence stolen from them. Some of the women had their faces buried in their hands and were being comforted by those around them. It was a heartbreaking scene. I began my talk and after awhile I no longer noticed the woman, stage right, signing for the deaf, or the woman in front translating into Danish. It was an odd feeling to stand before a full house and have two translators simultaneously sharing my message. My sister Sandy had come along on this trip with me as Ken had to stay home for medical reasons. Sandy felt the pull and was very helpful and supportive to the women at the reception afterward. It was an inspiring trip because we could feel that we were making a difference.

Emails and letters on lined school notebook paper began to come in from all over the world in broken English from girls who wanted to touch base with me and to know that there was support, that they were not alone. Those letters and emails are still coming in today. School girls tell me that *Cry the Darkness* is on their school reading lists. *Cry the* Darkness was acted out on a community college stage as a play. More and more frequently the theme of child sexual abuse appeared as a theme on prime time television dramas as well as on the big screen.

The work continued, in the mid and late 1990's a team of us, led by social activist, Colleen Campbell, became members of a group she formed called M.O.V.E. (Memory of Victims Everywhere). We testified at California state senate hearings to strengthen laws against offenders. We knocked on legislators' doors to plead our case. Doors were sometimes slammed in our faces. We were not always welcome as we were demanding change. We testified on Capitol Hill in Washington. We created documentaries and instructional videos to help law enforcement when dealing with victims. Several of us became spokespersons at rallies and conferences. I remember that at one conference I felt attacked. During the question-answer period, a tearful young man stood up and berated me, *"How could you? How could you turn in your own father?"* This was not the first time I had been castigated in public. There were those who wanted the entire subject to disappear. I heard the judgmental tone, "How could you!" "Do you forgive your father?" Is he still alive? Where was your mother? How dare you!" Mostly I just sucked up the vitriol and moved on. This was a type of defiance campaign – challenging the status quo and many were not that happy about it.

The famous McMartin preschool case whose trial ran from 1987 to 1990 helped to foment rage and awareness regarding child sexual abuse. Although there was never a conviction of the owners of the preschool, the trial added kindle to the fire of indignation. Our cause had the free world's attention. The dirty secret of the frequency of child sexual abuse was out in the open. One of the most gratifying roles I was allowed to play was to use my name and energy to help start some non-profit organizations devoted to helping women. In my own county a grassroots group was trying to open a shelter for victims of domestic violence. A non-profit organization was formed and Laura's House in Orange County was born.

For two years I went once a week for two hours and waited for teens to come in, victims of violence. I was a peer counselor and their stories made my heart stop; even girls as young as 15 were being beaten by their boyfriends. One girl came to me after her boyfriend had slammed her head against the curb of the street, severely injuring her. He had just broken out all the windows on her parents' Cadillac. The girl and I worked together until her family sent her out of State to keep her safe.

Another case of domestic violence was not as gratifying. Our case worker set up a young mother and her infant in temporary housing. When the social worker returned the next day to check on her, she found a note explaining that they went back home, because she was given the wrong brands of cigarettes and disposable diapers! My education into such matters grew during these years. Clearly it was not about the cigarettes. It must have been too traumatic for the mother to leave her life; the unknown being far more frightening than the known.

Twenty years later, Laura's House, to cite just one non-profit organization, serves 267 families per year with transitional housing, psychological, as well as legal counseling.

Claire Reeves, founder of Mothers Against Sexual Abuse, asked me to serve on her board of directors, as did the Child Abuse Mediation Center in Santa Barbara. Several Washington D.C. based non-profit organizations used my name and my speaking to pull in donations. There was a lot of work to be done. There is *still* a lot of work to be done. When I told my truth, maybe it was part of the healing process, maybe it was an outlet for my internal rage. Whatever it was, I have felt driven to use my horrible experience for good. I am doing what I can do to make the world safer for children and women.

As I write this, a new kind of sex scandal has appeared. Headline stories and robust television news reports are having a field day with statements by Todd Akin, a candidate running for a Republican senate seat. In his anti-abortion rhetoric he stated that "true female rape victims rarely get pregnant." He went on to more fully ignite the scandal by explaining "If it is a *legitimate* rape, the female body has ways to shut the whole thing down." (*L.A. Times,* August 22, 2012). Critics have picked up on this and reporters have learned that this thinking was a common belief in 17th century colonial America! It proves to me that there is still so much to do to shift the cultural attitudes toward more compassion for the powerless. I remember a class discussion once where a student, an older man, in my speech class informed us that "rape is the fault of the woman if she wears short skirts!" The women in my class went ballistic on him. But that comment shows that attitudes such as candidate Akin's continue to vilify the victim. Yes, there is still work to be done.

Across the years I wrote articles and published in professional journals and magazines and presented papers at professional conventions. In the process, I was particularly fascinated by the work of the 1990's showing permanent brain chemistry changes in victims of abuse like myself. Early studies show that those of us who suffer post traumatic stress disorder, had permanent changes resulting from being in a state of "hypervigilance" during the trauma. Research shows this to be true for war veterans and victims of disaster, as well as sexual abuse victims.

As I pursued my personal studies in the newly developing field of cognitive neuroscience, I learned what the use of functional MRI technology was allowing scientists to discover that we are in fact constantly growing *new* neurons in our brains. That is good news, suggesting that what was once considered "permanent" is probably not true. That has been a relief to me. I hated thinking that my brain cells were permanently tweaked!

As the years passed I could feel myself becoming more hostile toward sexual predators. The Jaycee Dugard case in which the 11 year-old California girl was kidnapped and held as a sexual slave for 18 years and even gave birth to two children from her captor, really bothered me. I hate that the Catholic Church itself has covered-up vast numbers of sexual abuse cases. I am horrified that teachers and coaches continue to steal innocence from children. Most recently the case against Penn State University football coach, Jerry Sandusky, has had seismic reverberations. Not just for him as the abuser, but for those involved in the failure to stop it. The sanctions against the university itself have been legendary.

A part of me is gratified that sexual abuse is out of the closet, another part struggles with how we can stop it once and for all. There is still so much work to be done, so I continue to push forward. I have been sitting on a United States Department of Justice, Office for Victims, TTAC, Technical Training and Assistance Center for victims of crime for the past nine years and I will continue to do this work. I am available to CNN when they need a subject matter expert, and I continue to share my story. Who better than those of us who know the horror of the abuse?

The media coverage in our case may have saved my father's wasted life. It was in November, 1994. I remember the day because I still have not resolved what I felt, and it has been almost 20 years. I was invited to be the keynote speaker for another healing conference.

I am not even sure now what organization it was, but I was to tell my story and to sign books. I recall that as the three hundred people took their seats in the large community room, I had scanned the crowd. The room had an odd vibe, a combination of adrenaline and fear. The listeners looked both eager and nervous at the same time as they stole glances toward me at the front of the room. Surely, they were scared of what feelings my talk would stir up.

Before the event began, a strong looking woman took me aside. "Donna, I am a guard at the prison facility in Eastern San Diego County where your father has been. I wanted you to know that when that cover story came out, I knew it would reveal his identity. I had the prison superintendent move him into protective custody. If the other inmates had gotten hold of him, I was afraid they would beat him to death. I heard that at one of the prisons he was pretty badly beaten up. These guys do NOT like child molesters!"

Her words stunned me. It brought to my full attention how completely I was blocking out where he was, what he was doing and what he was thinking. It was bad enough that he was constantly mailing thick letters printed in his precise engineering script from his cell. Clearly he had legal access to attorneys' contact information because he kept writing long letters to our attorney friends, long rambling arguments declaring his innocence. I had not read any of them, but I saw the bottom of one he had signed to our son. He signed it "Grandpa Boat" probably hoping to stir up any fond memories Rick might have retained from childhood. It did not work. My sons had nothing but contempt for him.

I finished the program for that group that day, talked to people, tried my best to give them hope and comfort, but part of my mind kept replaying the thought that they had to put dad into protective custody. I could not exactly read my feelings. That is probably why it has stayed so fresh in my memory. Actually, to this day I am not exactly clear about those feelings.

It was only two years later that our family received a call from the prison warden to tell us our father had died of leukemia. Sandy, concerned that this was yet another of our dad's lies, a ruse for us to let our guards down, called the prison morgue and had them identify markings on his body. She had to make sure that he was really dead. She had worried all along about her daughters' safety. She was not taking any chances. She withheld, even from us, the location of her girls' living situation. She worried that if he were released, there could be retribution and that he might unleash his fury on her girls. Even in his death, she was still deeply afraid of him.

The day the call came I shed some tears. After all I had been daddy's loyal girl. The tears were brief. I called Leanne and we shed some more. The sadness was for the fun memories we both had of my dad, all the help with the homework, the bumper cars at the amusement parks, the prom dress shopping, the constant encouragement as he told me that I could be anyone I wanted; I could do anything I set my mind to. Those tears mixed with the relief that it was really over. No more worries that he would be released, that we might need to hire body guards. I never had managed to wrap my head around how I would deal with a bodyguard in the classroom, in my office? Anyway, it was over.

Years later my sister Connie who had remained loyal to Dad during the trial and incarceration, confided to me that she cried until "there were no more tears." Sister Diana said, "When I heard that he had actually died, I shed about one tear and then smiled in relief. How sad is that? I remember being so poor, working nearly full-time and carrying a full load at the university and then having to pay the phone company a fee every month to keep my number unlisted. It was terrifying to think Dad could be released and park outside of my modest, but security-gated, apartment building with his gun under his seat. Ugh. I cannot believe we lived like that."

Each of us found a way to bring closure to our past. Once and for all it was over. It was finally really over.

CHAPTER THREE: FOOTPRINTS TO THE FUTURE

"By learning you will teach, by teaching you will learn."
Latin Proverb

As the 20th century flew toward its conclusion, its last two years offered something big: the chance for our family to lay down important footprints to our future. Incredibly, we experienced a perfect storm of opportunity for five future-shaping developments. Talk about synergy! When life's optimal circumstances collide with timing's perfect moment, amazing things can happened.

In this chapter and the next I would like to share a bit of them with you. Before your eyes you will see them appear of: wood and cement, paper and ink, flesh and blood, passport and airplane tickets.

As all of this unfolds, remember that quietly in the background our marrieds were working hard at their careers and raising their young families, as Ken ran his construction company and I was occupied with teaching and media appearances for *Cry the Darkness*. It was a dynamic time.

The back story to these new endeavors began in the early 1970's when Ken and I first heard about this place near Big Bear called Weesha Country Club. We understood that it was the old fashioned meaning of "country club," as it was very rustic, and actually situated in the "country" and boasted fishing not golf. Ken and I purchased a one bedroom river rock cabin in 1972.

Soon after that we invited our good friends Janet and Paul Tonkovich and their three small children to visit on one of the first weekends. They, too, fell in love with what felt like Weesha "magic;" serenity and the great outdoors. Within a few years they had secured their own cabin and we enjoyed raising our children together. It continues today, but it's 1998 when this occurred.

For decades we enjoyed summer weekend volleyball tournaments, Memorial Day parades featuring our little kids and their pets, tree-wassailing on freezing New Year's Eves, and more. On many cold New Year's holidays you could see us practically piled up together crammed into Janet's tiny living room or in ours. I remember thinking once that it felt like we were puppies, all together, enjoying the closeness of each other. I could not imagine a more wonderful way to spend weekends and vacations. Weesha has been a way of life for us. Our children and grandchildren cannot remember when we were not hiking, fishing and playing Frisbee Golf at Weesha.

It was a wholesome way to raise our families. However, it was not just about vacation fun, something profound took place in those early years while Janet and I followed our six offspring around the grounds. We became innocent recipients of a rich oral history. The other ten club members had mostly grown very senior and seeing the two of us young mothers somehow inspired them to share their stories of the early days of Weesha. At that time we were actually the only two young women in the club. They would stop us as our contingent headed for the river, children armed with fishing poles, to tell us about the old days. This was not an occasional occurrence.

The elders were quite concerned, almost determined, that we "girls" learn the club's history. My guess now as a grandmother myself is that they understood in a deeper way the rhythms of life and they wanted us to actually *know* the club's rich heritage. We were captivated by their stories. We were attentive students often quizzing each other about the facts that were told to us. Both Janet and I, great-granddaughters of California pioneers, had early-on embraced our own history and were proud to be California natives. Receiving these precious memories seemed natural to us.

So part of what I want to share with you came from this storytelling. When I look back across my life; my family, students, the adventures, the books, and painting, I know I will be proud of what turned out to be the securing of a piece of California history.

As young mothers we heard fascinating details of the club's horse and wagon beginnings, floods, and the tales of the glamorous goings on during the bootlegging eras at nearby Seven Oaks. Some of the most wonderful stories were of the mule trains that passed through nearby Clarke's Grade headed into Big Bear. In those days there were no highways, this was the only way into the beautiful lake valley from the west. We learned about bears too close to the tents, and rattlesnakes lurking in the tall grass under the apple trees. We understood that the founders of Weesha were Orange County pioneering ranchers and civic leaders. It was fascinating, but we were busy mothers raising our families, and, I was also a full- time college professor.

The summers came and went and the old-timers passed away or sold their interests in the club. After a decade or two Janet and I no longer played a quiz game about the history. We were wrapped up in our children who by then were young adults. We stopped thinking much about Weesha's past.

Then more than 20 years later, in the summer of 1997 a mind change occurred. I recall that Janet and I were walking toward her cabin from mine lamenting the fact that we "should have written it all down!" Oh how sorry we were as we shared some "should haves" with each other. Suddenly Janet exclaimed "Donna if you will write the story, I will help you research it!"

That was the starting shot for the writing of the historical book, *Whispering Waters: Historic Weesha and the Settling of Southern California.* Neither of us is the type to shrink from a task. We dug in like maniacs. Our memories still held much of the earlier oral histories but nothing was written down. To support what we already knew, we studied 88 years of club minutes and began to mine the archives and historical collections in the libraries and museums in Orange and San Bernardino Counties. When we learned of earlier members still being alive, we drove to interview them. We were hungry for anything related to our project. We quickly discovered that Weesha had the distinction of being the longest running private recreational camp in the state! All of this was hugely exciting for me because my academic discipline of communication rests on a foundation of oral narrative. This job was right up my alley.

Keep in mind that the events of those last years of the century were a combination of divergent circumstances. Take timing as one element. Our son Dan held fresh degrees in construction management and was eager and willing to help make the dream of expanding our mountain cottage into a reality. For my part, I was granted a sabbatical leave for half of the 1998 school year which allowed me to work more closely with Dan, now commander-in-chief of the construction project, and I had time to continue the work of researching. In addition the family was at a point to be able to finance the project.

While I wrote, Dan and his team broke ground for our 3600 square foot addition in May of 1998. This was after an arduous effort on Dan's part just getting the appropriate permits to add-on to a nearly 100 year-old rock cabin far into the mountains of the San Bernardino National Forest. It was a bureaucratic nightmare. In spite of the hurdles, Dan made the entire project, which was the largest construction project the current members of our club had experienced, look fairly easy. It was anything but that. For example when they dug the foundation trenches the ground was still frozen. They had to wait until it thawed, and then it became so wet that other problems arose. It was difficult to make progress.

Another of the challenging aspects of the 15 month-long project was the task of getting building materials across the Santa Ana River crossing. A truck had to cross through the water and then drive on a muddy unpaved road to reach our cabin, plus the major problem of finding construction workers willing to work so far away.

We had pretty good timing and a fair bit of luck for these two big projects. But it takes more than timing. It also takes sheer determination and lots of energy and commitment. We had that and we needed it. Dan would build while Janet and I would write. Dan and the workers faced snow, rain, frigid temperatures and harsh conditions. The project required a gigantic new septic tank which had to be hauled up narrow mountain roads to the 6000 foot elevation and then brought down an even more narrow, winding road to our site at 5200 feet elevation. Then it had to be driven through the river crossing. Massive steel support beams were required to span the two story 30-foot wide structure. Those too had to be lugged up the mountain roads, as did concrete trucks filled to capacity, and delivery trucks loaded with lumber.

On our frequent trips up to the camp, Dan would supervise the construction while I explored the property with new eyes, trying to confirm what Janet and I had been discovering. The day I actually *found* the site of the 3000–watt Delco Electric Lighting Plant described in the club's 1925 Minutes, was a big thrill. For those pioneers, the electric plant meant no more kerosene! It was run by the "drop" of the river water. When we found its ancient foundation, water pipes still attached, I could not believe that it lay within 20 feet of our cabin. Our children had often played on its cement pad, never dreaming what it had once been. During the Delco days each member-family had to pay $10 for one single electrical outlet to be installed in their cabins. The members dreamed of some exterior lights, but they proved to be too expensive.

So as Dan struggled to find workers for our remote place, Janet and I continued our research. We came to understand that this piece of California history had *never* before been captured. It, like the construction, was an ambitious project, but we were all in. If I am beginning to drive you crazy with, as my grandchildren would say, TMI, (too much information), just skip ahead. I only share this to give you a glimpse into my thinking, as it is my brain that has allowed me to leave my childhood devastation far behind. I believe that when we are passionate about things, when we are in the flow of important projects, the pain of loss or of the past is remediated.

Our passion to preserve this unique piece of Americana was amplified by the fact that Janet and Paul actually *owned* the original log cabins built in 1888 by pioneer Edwin Ball and his wife Jennie. When we obtained copies of the 1897 homestead deed on the 132 acres we knew we had stumbled onto some of the settling of the "wild west." Prior to 1888, the property had been a flourishing operation known as Oakdale Ranch. Ball sold apples, vegetables, and dairy products to the well know Seven Oaks Resort, a mile up the road. This was long before Big Bear became a destination. The Balls were also one of the earliest pioneering families to settle the Redlands area located 50 miles from Weesha. In Redlands, they opened the first grocery store, the first hotel, Pioneer House, the city's first restaurant. Mr. Ball served as the first policeman in Redlands, as a game warden, and as county assessor. The story was rich and possibly worth its own book.

After Edwin's death in 1900, in the cabin now owned by Janet and Paul, Ball's wife and son ran the ranch for seven more years. In 1910 it was sold to Orange County rancher and community leader, Charles Wagner. Charles' wife complained about the loneliness and isolation of the log cabin. To bring in new life, they quickly sold off interests to their relatives and friends. In 1910 it was chartered as the Weesha Country Club, Inc. and continues to be the longest held privately owned recreational corporation in California.

The early club members were at the center of the vast Riverside and Orange County citrus industry and as such were some of the most powerful families in all of Southern California. They developed improvements in the Valencia orange and invented new methods of crop fumigation. They influenced rail lines as thousands of railcar loads of their oranges were shipped to hungry eastern markets each year. Riverside and Orange counties were booming.

Our appetite for information grew as we learned more about those early families. Janet's great grandparents were Orange County pioneering ranchers. I have a photo of them in front of their orchard in La Habra in 1900. Her grandparents also worked the ranch and had known some of the early Weesha families. My great grandparents grew walnuts on what would become Disneyland's parking lot and eventually California Adventure. As we dug and studied, it became clear to me that to do justice to the history, the story had to be told within the context of the settling of Southern California and so the project grew.

There is more. One day while sitting at my computer, I recalled a big discovery my children had made. They were little, so it had to be in the early 1970's. I remember it vividly; they had wandered away looking for more snow for a snowball fight when suddenly they yelled to Ken and me to "come quickly!" None of us could believe that they had found an artifact of such significance, a prehistoric mortar rock. For weeks we talked of the indigenous people who once inhabited our area. The children shared about it in school. It was a very big thing.

And then, 20 years later in the 1990's during a family hike, not far from our cabin it happened again! We came upon another grinding rock but this one was a large boulder with many pockets. I knew that the Los Angeles Natural History Museum was very proud of its large photograph of a mortar rock, and this one was many times more impressive than that one.

Those memories got me excited about the ancients who had lived at our place so long ago. I could envision them in the morning light grinding acorns in that rock along the river, preparing their breakfast. My imagination would not let go of them. I wanted to include them in my story. The name "Weesha" was thought to be a Serrano or Gabrielano word meaning "whispering waters." I wanted to find out more about the Native Americans and that meant even additional research, a more complicated project.

Knowing this was going to require more of my sabbatical time, I proposed to my college district that this oral history be part of my sabbatical leave project. They granted my wish and so through most of 1998 I typed and researched while Janet sent me bundles of copies of documents. We produced a three hundred page book which included photos of some of the original members. Club members and their families purchased copies and we donated others to library and museum collections. We had some wonderful reviews and enjoyed the fact that the famous Southern California historian John Robinson enthusiastically praised our work. We were pleased with the final product and happy to move on. However that was not to be the case.

INCREDIBLE DISCOVERIES

Once the book was published, an excitement for the old days took hold. As interested parties read it, they began to think about the old suitcases in their attics and trunks in their garages. Early on we had called upon our neighbors and those associated with Weesha for support materials, but we met with only minimal success. Perhaps we were not taken seriously, but with a handsome book in hand, enthusiasm spread and suddenly new materials were made available to us.

Before I tell you about our incredible "finds" you need to understand why they were a big deal. For years Ken and our children and I hiked the Upper Santa Ana River Trail above Weesha to an abandoned Boy Scout camp that had once been the flourishing Stetson Ranch. Yes, the Stetsons of the big hat. By the time we visited, it was nothing more than a "ghost ranch." However that fact delighted the children even more as they explored its dilapidated buildings and posed in front of the old outhouse. I took pictures of the carvings in the cement which declared that "Mary of the Mountain" had once lived there. That was at the turn of the last century. Mary Stetson was one of my heroes. I had read about her riding bareback through the mountains with her long red hair flowing behind her. She intrigued me. In my heart of hearts I imagined myself a lot like Mary. I had in fact learned how to ride a horse during our first summer at Weesha, bareback.

One morning over coffee Janet shared a story about Mary Stetson with me. Janet recalled a spooky encounter one dark winter day back in the 1970's. On that damp and foggy late afternoon, she thought she heard a faint knock on her cabin door. The knock persisted. Very cautiously she opened the door, knowing just how isolated they were. Janet described the incident to me:

I opened the door and there stood a very tiny old woman. She looked ancient as she croaked something out to me. She was weak and cold, and she was being held up by a man in dirty over-alls. I immediately invited them in. This odd looking couple explained that she was Mary Stetson and that she had been Ray Hale's bride and once occupied the white cabin perched above the apple orchard. She explained that her great wish, for one last time, was to drink out of the Forsee Creek. I gave them each a glass of water while they warmed themselves by the fire. The strange man explained that he once lived in the stone control house outside of Weesha's gate and that his father had been a Weesha caretaker and that he came from a long line of Weesha caretakers. There was more visiting. The man explained that the Weesha folks would send messages in balloons to him and they would float down to his cabin. Then suddenly they both stood up. He said, "I'm taking Mary back to her rest home." And they left. It was a very odd visit.

It might have been an odd meeting but in recalling it, we were one step closer to the past.

We began getting calls from former Weesha people who wanted us to see their old albums and boxes of yellowing documents. We became the lucky recipients of the most amazing collections: the marriage certificate for Mary Stetson who indeed did come to Weesha as a bride, as well as her hand-written story published in Sunset Magazine about her famous hat family. There were also grant deeds, letters, and incredible old photos of life as it was lived in the Upper Santa Ana River Valley long before Highway 38 existed and Big Bear became popular.

We even found a photo of the niece of famous Californio, land-grant holder, Marco Forster. The Forster family had owned much of what is now south Orange County since the 1830's. Don Juan Forester, Marco's father, once owned the Mission San Juan Capistrano. Ken and I enjoyed sharing that old photo with Marco's great grandson, our friend Tony. In fact all of our children and now five of our grandchildren have been or will be Marco Forster Middle School students.

Our book was finished, but how could we ignore this cache of precious documents? We just couldn't. Both Janet and I understood that if we did not capture this information, it would probably be lost forever. We could not have that, so two years later we published a second book which preserved our newly acquired treasures: *A Chronicle of Historic Weesha and the Upper Santa Ana River Valley.*

And so you can see how captivated I was with those writing projects. As the pages reeled out of me, our son, builder Dan, kept at it. More perfect timing, our former employee Jerry met with Ken and explained that he and his wife were moving back to California. Jerry is a master mason. Ken offered Jerry the opportunity to be a part of our mountain project. He and his wife, Jean, moved into the construction site to facilitate its completion. Artistic by nature, Jerry added exquisite finishing details. He hand-carved our mantel and included shapes of leaves found on the trees of the property; he took great care in choosing each river rock as he placed it in the fireplace surround. He tiled the bathrooms and all the kitchen counters. When he got to the front patio he worked his magic with more river rock. The construction site was turning into an art project and a beautiful home. We in the family were itching to move in. Finally in August of 1999, Dan gave the go-ahead. We were thrilled to take possession the next weekend!

So you witnessed the cement and wood become a home, the old stories turn from ink and paper into two history books. However, I promised you that *five footprints to the future* were laid down during that time. Footprint number three was flesh and blood.

***

Quietly in the background during those projects a beautiful romance had been unfolding which I have not told you about. Dan had known Lisa Brown, the daughter of one of the Weesha families since he was a little boy. Lisa remembers Dan as a determined five year-old fisherman. She smiles when she recalls seeing him at Weesha decked out in his cowboy boots, fishing pole in his right hand, tackle box in his left, heading to the river. As casual friends and neighbors, Dan and Lisa knew of each other as they enjoyed summer after summer of parades and volleyball games. Then suddenly in young adulthood on a Memorial Day weekend in the mid 1990's, Dan *really* noticed Lisa! He could talk of little else.

They began dating and after awhile, whispered plans about the future began to emerge. Our family was elated to learn that Lisa would become a part of us. One day, I was honored to be invited to accompany my youngest son as he shopped for an engagement ring. I think we all felt the excitement as Dan began his own family. We were moving forward.

Our research showed that no other such romance had ever blossomed between club members across Weesha's entire history. Dan and Lisa became known as the "royal couple," the "true Weesha romance." By the end of the summer of 1999, they had finalized their wedding plans and September promised to be an eventful month.

WEDDING BELLS

On a drizzly summer afternoon in September, we witnessed our last child exchanging vows with his fiancé, the beautiful young woman, Lisa Brown. Dan and Lisa chose a wonderful church overlooking the Pacific. It was a remarkable ceremony. One of my fondest moments was when four-year-old flower girl, Jillian, managed to get all the way down the aisle, only to be overtaken by an attack of shyness. A laugh erupted across the congregation as little Jillian suddenly ran back to the safety of her mother who was seated nearby.

That morning when I awoke I saw that it was raining. I became worried about the outdoor reception planned for later that day. When I shared my concerns with Lisa she replied, "Donna, don't worry. It will clear. I know that it will be beautiful."

And true to her word it was. The gorgeous fresh-air reception was held at lovely Rancho Capistrano in San Juan Capistrano. It included a seven piece band which allowed for a lively evening of dancing and fun.

I will never forget the special touch Lisa put on the party. Instead of the traditional bridal bouquet and garter toss, Lisa began a new tradition. She had the emcee invite all the married couples to the dance floor, they danced and slowly the emcee excused anyone married 5 years or less, 10 years or less and finally he got to 40 years and the tension began to build between Ken's Aunt Cam and Uncle Jack and another few couples. By the 55 year mark they were the sure winners; the last couple to remain dancing. There was a huge round of applause and then Lisa presented Aunt Cam with the bridal bouquet.

There was picture-taking and congratulations for them. It was a beautiful way to celebrate love and marriage. For years since Cam would describe that gesture as one of the most meaningful and outstanding moments in her life. I am so impressed with Lisa for doing that. Her act touched Cam's life in a spiritual way.

Moving ahead 13 years to the summer of 2012, Aunt Cam and Uncle Jack had passed away, but their beautiful granddaughter, Lila, used that same tradition at her wedding. During the reception she invited the married couples up for the wedding dance. Ken pulled me into his arms and we began to move. After five minutes of dancing, the emcee began to excuse couples. We kept dancing; 20 years, 30 years, 40 years, 45 years. Finally there was just one other couple dancing next to us. The party goers watched with mounting excitement. Ken and I eyed the other couple. They looked sort of old to us. *Maybe they have been married longer?...* Ken put me into a dip, as I bent back I made eye contact with Julie. She was beaming; her big green eyes were alive with anticipation. She seemed thrilled by the drama unfolding in front of her and for the tiniest of seconds I wondered what it might be like to come from an intact family....to be the child of happily married parents, but then Ken twirled me around in a big spin.

As the suspense continued we kept dancing. We sneaked another peek at our competition. We looked at each other, *can we outlast them?* The spectators seemed to be holding their breath. The announcer yelled out, "Forty-six years!" With that our competitors walked off the floor! We smiled. We did not even need our 48 years. Everyone crowded around us clapping and laughing. The bride and groom came for hugs and then the bride presented me with her bouquet. I was beaming as I thought of Aunt Cam and her most special day. Lisa had started something wonderful in our family and I will remember it as her legacy. I smile when I think of it and especially how much happiness she brought to Aunt Cam.

CHAPTER FOUR: MORE FOOTPRINTS

"Today I close the door to the past, open the door to the
future, take a deep breath and step through."
Unknown

It would be easier to follow my story if just one event at a time happened, but that is not how life works. Yes, we moved into our mountain home, our two history books were published, and Dan and Lisa bought a house. It was all good as life continued on course. The court case and my difficult childhood seemed far in the past. Many opportunities were presented for me to speak out against child abuse, to work to toughen laws to protect children, and I was actively involved with a Federal group known as TTAC, a Training and Technical Assistance Center through the Justice Department's Office for Victims of Crime.

One of my activities was to help other activists in completing a DVD for law enforcement, it was to help mentor crime victims. Ken traveled with me on many of these out-of-town weekends, but his energy seemed to be lagging. I recall that we were in Miami for some meetings and Ken was not up for going out in the evening, even for a little walk. This was not like him. Something was wrong.

After that Florida trip, he went for tests. It was determined that something bad was going on within his large intestine. The doctors could not discover what was wrong. Ken was hospitalized while the doctors ran intravenous antibiotics into his system. He was not responding to the high doses of drugs. In fact he seemed to be growing weaker. One particular night at the hospital when he was struggling with pain and fear, he had fallen asleep and my sister Sandy came by to check on us. I remember expressing out loud the terrible worry I was having, "Sis, am I going to *lose* him?" Sandy did not know, neither did the doctors. We prayed a lot. The days were long. Finally, the doctor determined that Ken was strong enough to undergo exploratory surgery on his colon. They had to look around. They did not know what they would find. No promises were made.

Dan sat with me during the long and terrifying hours of Ken's surgery. Our greatest fear was that the doctors would discover cancer in his large intestine and close him up and tell us they were sorry. Dan and I sat in silence. Hours later the surgeon came out. Silently, he led us to his office. I was thankful to have my strong young son standing next to me. We were braced for the worst.

The doctor began, "We removed 18 inches of his colon. It was infected. We think we got it all. He should be okay." Dan and I each exhaled a deep breath as tears of relief clouded my eyes. My worst fear, of losing Ken, was lifted from me. Dan and I felt the heavy burden of worry slide away from our shoulders. I could not even imagine having to go through life without my Ken. . .

That incident became a scary wake-up call for Ken about smelling the roses and not taking everything to heart, or in this case to his gut. He knew he needed to lighten up. During our quiet-time talks we grew even closer. We had many heart to hearts during his long recovery. I felt safe enough to share one of my truths with him, that an important life's goals which I had pretty much put on hold was to see the world. I confessed that I was worried that I might miss my chance. It was a serious goal and I saw that I was moving quickly through the decades of my life.

The year before, when Ken and I had gone on a book tour to Norway, the trip proved to me how much I had been stuffing my desire to travel. I had subjugated myself to the family, which was fine, but I felt I was running out of time.

I shared with him, in a new way, how much that trip had meant to me and showed me how much I did not know about other places and people. I even confessed to him that before we left for Oslo, I researched how the people dressed in Scandinavia. Somehow in my fantasies I was thinking about the nomadic tribes in the very north and the animal skins they wore as they followed their herds around the North Pole. I am embarrassed to share that, but it is true. I was quite surprised to learn that they wore western clothes!

Through whispered sentences I even told Ken that when I knew for sure that we were going to Norway, on the day my new passport arrived which had expired 15 years earlier, I put on my long winter coat and pulled my new roller suitcase around the house! I did it for a long time. I was practicing walking through the airport!

After Norway, the Danish publisher of my book had invited me for a spring book tour saying that they would take care of the Copenhagen details of the trip. Hearing all this and knowing he was too weak to go with me, Ken insisted that I follow through with my plans. Sandy volunteered to go with me. The first part of the trip was easily executed as my book editor picked us up at the airport and took care of us. It was a whirlwind of media appearances and public speaking. The second leg of the trip was a bit more challenging. Sandy and I were determined to visit nearby Sweden, the original home of our great-great grandparents. However, we were such novice travelers that we did not foresee the challenges two women who did not speak Swedish would have driving alone across the country.

We left Copenhagen by ferry to Malmo, Sweden. After the short boat ride to Sweden, the boat docked and Sandy and I rolled our suitcases across the street to the Avis car rental office and were off, heading for a week in Stockholm. I was not sophisticated enough to know to call a travel agent or even to sign up with a tour operator, so I did it the hard way. I bought a Swedish guide book and used my fax machine to make reservations. This was before the Internet.

When all was done, like many other intrepid travelers, Sandy and I had a marvelous adventure staying in out-of-the-way places. For a few nights we stayed in an ancient monastery and awoke to the chanting of monks across the courtyard. Other nights found us in an historic hunting lodge that had belonged to a long ago nobleman. During morning coffee we watched deer grazing nearby. All of that was great fun.

However, there were some challenges, like the time we had lines of angry drivers backed up behind us at the car park because we had no idea how to work the automated pay station, or when we were nearly out of gas and could not figure out how to use the gas pump! Reading the Swedish instructions was no help. With the gas gauge running dangerously low we were forced to go gas station hopping, hoping to find one with a human who could lend assistance. Happily we found such a person before our car ran out of gas. Yes, some challenges, but that experience proved to be a training ground for me. It gave me the seeds of confidence to continue with my travel adventures.

The success of that trip inspired me to make more travel plans. I invited my 15 year-old niece, Keely, the girl for whom we had to intervene against my father, to accompany me to Ireland the next summer. The trip was a test of my love and patience but that is a story for another time.

And so you see, the fourth footprint was laid for the future: World travel. With passport in hand and plane ticket, I could finally realize this part of my life's dream. It was happening and I was joyous about it.

However, in spite of these amazing blessings; there continued to be a solemn hole in my heart that I was determined to close. I had to find my missing baby brother. I have a very clear memory of watching his little unborn feet kicking against his mother's abdomen. I was nine-and-a-half years old. It was 1952 and I was plenty old enough to remember. I loved to put my hands against our babysitter, Bernie's, tummy and feel the baby move inside. I know that I was very excited about this new baby. I dreamed about playing with the baby.

On the day that Bernie went into labor and Dad took her to the hospital I was very excited. A new infant to play with! I had so much fun with our half-sister Cee Cee. She was a big part of my life. I had been very careful to keep the secret about who her real daddy was, our dad. I was very good at keeping secrets! Plus, I was an experienced babysitter and knew I would be a big help with this new baby. A few days later when Dad brought Bernie home from the hospital, all that changed. They did not bring the baby home. They told me rather matter-of-factly the baby was a boy and that they had given him away. I remember thinking *gave him away, you GAVE AWAY our baby?* I never was able to process that event. I wondered if they would have given him away if he had been a *girl.* I had so loved to touch Bernie's tummy and feel him move and kick. I felt connected to him. Given away? That had troubled me across my life; unfinished business and it also revealed a harsh reality about my father's callous approach to our family life. This act became yet another secret demanding my silence.

LOST AND THEN FOUND

I will never forget the day when there was the *real* possibility of finally finding our lost brother. Across the years I had argued with Dad about searching for him. He brushed me off and assured us that he had long ago hired detectives and learned that our brother had died in Viet Nam. Dad wanted the subject dropped. The case was closed, but some of us believed in our hearts that one day we would find our missing sibling.

Later, as an adult, Chad had taken up the search, but it had proven to be a dead end. Our brother Trey, had a neighbor, Nicky, who was a member of an underground birth family search network. He asked her to begin the hunt for our "given away" brother.

It was the Wednesday evening just before the start of the long Thanksgiving weekend, 1999. I had been watching the 6 o'clock news when the phone rang. It was my brother Trey. "Donna, I have the phone number of our brother. He's not in Florida as we had thought."

"Trey, really? Where is he?" I asked as my heart skipped a beat. I had felt breathless ever since Trey's neighbor began the serious search. I had been filled with both hope and dread.

"He's in the San Fernando Valley."

"Right here? I bet he has been here all along. Was your neighbor able to discover his name?"

"He is *Dominic. Dominic Anthony* and he is married with two kids." Trey's voice was subdued. We both understood that we were standing at a precipice.

Thoughts whirled around in my head. *Right here? I have two more nieces or nephews. Trey found our brother!* I was shaking.

"Are you going to call when we get off?" My emotions were running wild; my heart thumped as it responded to its sudden adrenaline jolt.

"I have a bad cold. I'm just not up to it," answered Trey.

"I'll do it. I'll do it right now!" I responded urgently. "What's the number?" Trey shared the precious digits and after a few more minutes we signed off.

This would be a forever moment. I would never forget this day. Ironically, that very day in class I had shown my relationship students the film *A Family Thing* in which Robert Duvall discovers he was not the white guy he thought he was, that he had been adopted, and he was half black. Duvall learns he has a brother, Raymond, played by James Earl Jones, living in Chicago. The story is the drama of Robert Duvall meeting his half-brother.

My intuition was on high alert. I knew that by placing this call I could be severely disrupting my brother's life. I pondered my approach. I did not want to make a mess of this. I calmed myself by taking some deep breaths and slowly exhaling. My mind ran through a variety of scenarios. If I were lucky enough to get him on the phone, I would introduce myself. With the film freshly in my mind I understood that my call might not be welcome. Our brother might not even know he had been adopted. This had the potential of setting off a disastrous chain of events that might seriously upset his life. There might be consequences lurking beneath the surface I could not even imagine.

I sucked in a deep breath and placed the call. My hands trembled as I pushed in the numbers. More random possibilities floated across my mind: if he answered, if his wife or child answered, if I got a message machine…If…If…?

I finished punching in the number. The phone rang once, twice, three times. I thought of hanging up. Four times. My heart raced. The answering machine picked up.

The beep and I was on! I chose my words carefully. "This is Donna Friess. I live here in Orange County. We want to talk to Dominic about a personal matter." I left my phone number. I hoped that by saying "we" I would not cause a problem with his wife hearing my feminine voice. I knew that if a woman left a mysterious message for Ken about a "personal matter" my own hypervigilant antennae would go on alert!

I was a ball of nerves. I did my best to calm myself. I knew there was nothing more to be done for right now. I forced myself to chill. You have gotten to know me pretty well. I am not one who does "chill" that well but I tried. We were heading to the mountains for the holiday weekend. I purposely left the answering machine off at home. I sensed that letting this devolve into a phone tag situation would be wrong. My imagination ran wild dreaming up what this truly long lost brother might be like

A distinctive family trait that many of us siblings share is the almond-shaped slanting eyes of our forbearers. A photo of my grandmother's father, Joseph, hangs on the wall in my hall and reveals that he too had such eyes. People often comment that when Trey and I laugh, our eyes narrow to slits. We are used to this genetic reminder of the Mongol invasion of Europe. I frequently enjoy stretching my arm out next to the Vietnamese girls who do my nails to show them that my skin tone is more yellow than theirs. They just shake their heads in wonder at how strange I am. All they have to do is look at my blonde hair and blue eyes to see the European genes in me, but I am clear about the yellow cast to my skin and the slant to my eyes. Those young manicurists may not understand my English very well or what I am implying, but as a student of world history I am fascinated by Genghis Khan's invading Mongol hordes in the 1200's. Their successful march across China and then Europe under Genghis' son Kublai Khan, as they raped and pillaged, ensured their genetic imprint. Showing off my yellow skin tones is one of the strange ways I entertain myself.

In my heart I knew that it was the right time for us to gather this missing sibling into the fold. We were all adults, but was it right for him? Would he want to join us? He might not. He might not want to know about our father. A part of me longed to finish this chapter in my book of life. I was the only one of us old enough to remember him and the day he *did not come home from the hospital.* With him we would be eight, *Pieces of Eight*; a complete set. I liked that.

The last of the five footprints into the future, this one flesh and blood as well, was put in place with the phone calls. It was a Monday afternoon, November 27, 1999. I was at home. The long holiday weekend had seemed longer than ever with that unfinished call hanging in the air. When I had gone to school that morning I made sure that the answering machine was turned on. As I taught my students that day, the thoughts of Dominic reeled around my mind. I could hardly wait to get home to the answering machine.

"You have two unheard messages" rasped the robotic voice of our machine. My heart danced a little extra beat. I felt a pang of pleasure, then fear. *Let's get this over with* I chided myself as I pushed the play button on the machine.

"This is Cathy Anthony returning your call."

I was stunned, but without a second's hesitation, I dialed the number. She answered after the first ring. I identified myself in the same mysterious way I had in the original phone message. "This is Donna Friess. I am only here in Orange County. Is Dominic available to come to the phone?"

"No, I'm sorry. He's working. He'll be home after five." She responded.

"Could you have him return my call when he gets in? It is a personal matter."

Suddenly she blurted out, "We know Dom is adopted!" Clearly she had her own intuition about what this mystery matter might be about.

"Dom" I thought. He has a nickname! How wonderful! How like Donna it sounds. Dom and Donna.

Whoa! That did it. The flood gates were opened and we chatted openly for over an hour. She poured out the entire story. I learned that Dom had only recently discovered that he was adopted. His adoptive father told him upon the death of his adoptive mother. She had gone to great lengths to keep his adoption a secret, wearing a pillow under her clothes to simulate pregnancy. Secrets on top of secrets. Dom had been kept away from any relatives who might have revealed his mother's deception. For over 40 years the reality of his birth was kept from him. Cathy, my "new" sister-in law told me more. She told me they had two young children, a boy and a girl, ages four and seven.

I invited them to meet us at our home and they accepted. The next weekend we met at my house on a Saturday night. We kept the sibling group fairly small, Cee Cee, Chad, Trey and Connie. Even the "small" group could seem like a lot of people and we did not want to overwhelm him or his family. That first visit is still so vivid in my memory. In they came, Dom looking a whole lot like Trey, with his own set of slanting eyes. He also took after his mother, Bernie. I could not take my eyes off his beautiful young children. The familial resemblance was startling; they could be interchangeable with our kids and grandkids. The boy, John, was a replica of Trey when he was little, complete with the blonde hair, slanting eyes and long waist. The little girl, Kayla, was beautiful with sandy blonde hair and sparkling eyes. Both children seemed hungry to have more family members. I had gifts for them. That first dinner meeting whirled by. Dom brought his baby book, eager to bring us up to speed in his life. There was absolutely no doubt that we had found our brother!

When we finally settled down, Dom explained, "After my mother died, my dad took me out to dinner and told me about my birth, that I was adopted, and that he had the attorney's contact number if I wanted to find you all. I knew that somehow you would find me. I told that to my dad. 'They will find me.' I said that to him. I had a kind of knowing, a strong feeling about it." He paused and took a long look at us. "I mean it. I *knew* you would find me."

Across the long years I had fought the loss of him, wondered where he was and if he were okay. I had never really focused on the fact that he probably had children, that I had lost out on them too. My words here cannot express the feeling of completion and peace I felt and continue to feel from finding this brother after almost fifty years. It was incredible and has divided time for me; before Dom and after.

And so that was the beginning of having this wonderful man and his family in our lives. That was all it took, one simple phone call and we set into place another important footprint to the future.

***

Ten Years later, as I shook sleep from my head I realized that today was Dom's 60th birthday. A smile played across my lips as I became fully awake. It was the first actual birthday party I had ever hosted for him, and the first ever birthday present I had gotten for him. After my coffee that morning I sent him this email.

Dom, I am so thrilled that you are coming. Today is a celebration for us of having you in our lives. Yes, 3:00 p.m. I am getting set up right now.

It is a vivid memory for me as a nine-and-a-half-year-old that you were kicking in your mom's tummy. I loved you then, was horrified that you did not come home with them from the hospital, and love you still. It feels like our pieces of eight are finally together. All sibs coming today except Trey who is out of town. See you soon. Love, sister Donna

I recall that the August day was clear and bright, the roses were in full bloom and the pool was warm. It was wonderful to have everyone together for this occasion. I remember that I felt torn between happy and sad feelings that day. I was happy that we found him after all those years and sorry at the same time that I missed 48 birthdays with him.

A NEW MILLENNIUM

You see so many life-changing events were occurring just as the millennia changed. In the months leading up to this year 2000, I noticed a palpable excitement in the air everywhere I went. Part of it had to do with all that was going on in our private lives, but there was more. When I considered the thousands of years of humanity that had come before us, I was awed that I got be among the seven billion on the planet who would get to experience, not just a new century but a new millennium! I even liked saying it, *millennium*. It seemed to offer so much promise. When I thought of what the next 1000 years meant in terms of the changes for humanity, I had to smile. I was enchanted. I wanted to peek over the top and look ahead. I felt optimistic for the future, but millions of others across the planet did not.

In the months leading up to the change in centuries dire predictions declared that there would be massive global infrastructure failures. A Bug, a Millennium Bug, also known as Y2K, would fell our world's traffic control systems, business operations, such as banking, would be paralyzed, and the world now so dependent on computers would be in chaos. Billions of dollars were spent in the months leading up to midnight December 31st, as the computer world dealt with the fact that software was geared to read years in two digit combinations. The fear was that when long-working systems went from 99 to 00, the numbers would become invalid. The computers would shut down. The news outlets reported mind numbing stories leading up to all this, but except for minor glitches, the world continued on its normal axis as the calendar changed. No power grids were out, no contaminated drinking water, no planes crashing in the sky. Our lives continued on.

It will be no surprise to you that our family in its typical energetic style embraced the future. As was our tradition, we gathered at Weesha for the millennium event. Of course that was one occasion that *had* to be a freeze frame. As I said, changing millennia felt mysterious to me, huge somehow.

We believed the next century would be a great one. Our little fishing club would not slip quietly into this new era. We wanted to C.E.L.E.B.R.A.T.E! So on New Year's Eve, December 31st, 1999, we put forth a more elaborate effort than ever to make this event unforgettable. Our tradition had been to have a club-wide progressive dinner, but for this auspicious occasion we pitched in to make it bigger. This year, we caroled, ate delicious food and enjoyed twinkle lights sparkling against a white blanket of snow as we paraded from one cabin to another singing our hearts out in the winter cold. We would not be daunted by the media frenzy of fear. It was wonderful family fun with the children trying to stay awake until midnight. The culmination was our midnight tradition of wassailing the trees which Janet had begun years before as a way to celebrate her own Nordic heritage. This custom requires that the band of us who have gathered sprinkle a wassail mixture upon the branches of the bare apple tree as we sing out the ancient wassail song. I am not sure that we ever inspired the trees to deliver a high spring yield, but it was fun to try. The evening ended with a bonfire which helped to warm our freezing hands. It was a luscious and memorable way to usher in the new calendar and some new family members.

Three and a half weeks later, more excitement burst forth. Jenny delivered a beautiful little baby girl on January 25 named Emily. This was daughter number three for our son Rick and his wife Jenny. The next month Julie and Justin welcomed a nine-pound boy named James. Dan and Lisa were not to be left out of the parenthood jackpot and they too welcomed their first little girl, Lauren into the world. What a start of this century for Ken and me, three new grandchildren for 2000!

THE DAY OF INFAMY

If only my story could be just of travel, building projects, finding relatives, and babies, but that is not the case. The terrible events of that worst September day of 2001, when our world changed forever, remain vivid in my memory. I had taken the dogs out for our usual two mile walk. It was a hot day and I was preparing to take my shower before getting ready for school when the phone rang. It was my sister Sandy. "Donnie, turn on the TV, the World Trade Center has been hit by an airplane. It's bad, sis!" Her voice choked off with a sob.

Immediately, I switched on the news to see grey smoke pouring from high up in the WTC. I called to Ken. We could not believe what we were seeing. It took all my will power to tear myself from the tumultuous scene that was unfolding on the television, but I had students waiting.

Upon arriving at the college, rumors were raging. The news had reported that an airplane had crashed into the Pentagon and another into a field in the East. It was thought that a plane was heading for nearby Los Angeles International Airport. The students were panicked. There were rumors of a sighting of a low flying airplane over neighboring Cerritos where many of the students lived.

Classes were not cancelled. It was the responsibility of us teachers to keep order by maintaining our routine. I will never forget what it felt like to walk into that classroom to face the tear-stained faces. Many of the students were holding each other. I took a deep breath. I felt wobbly inside myself, but knew I had a job to do.

In a somber voice I directed the students to form a circle. It seemed to calm them to have something to do. As we gathered together, I shared what I had learned on the news. One by one they began to tell what they had heard and seen. As the conversation continued around the room, they began to share their feelings, their fears. It was a long day and by day's end we knew that Southern California was not under attack. In fact it was just the opposite as planes were grounded across the country. The sky was devoid of airplanes and their sounds. It was peaceful and unsettling at the same time.

For the next few days, I led the students in that cathartic exchange. It seemed to be healing, but in private I cried for the aunt who had so excitedly bought airline tickets to take her little four-year old niece to Disneyland only to crash into the Trade Center; for the young fireman, Dan was his name, who went back into the tower to try to help more people, only to be crushed when the building toppled down on him. I cried for all of them. It was a bad time for the nation and it burned at my heart. We lost some 3000 people that day. Innocent, hard working Americans. Their average age was only 40. It was difficult for me not to worry about all the children who lost their mom or dad that day. It still hurts. When *Time Magazine* published its tribute edition to those who were lost, I read every word, again and again. Somehow I did not want to forget them.

A FULL HOUSE

So much was going on at once. After the terrorist attacks daily routines finally resumed. Americans persevere. Life within our family was no exception. We continued to experience our own population growth with our three millennium babies and adding Dom and his family to our big gang. We enjoyed a full house. There was a lot going on and we chose to celebrate life. This was accomplished through elaborate and noisy Christmas parties and frequent family gatherings. One of our favorite traditions has been the Catalina summer reunion. It started for me with Leanne's family. I then brought it to my family, spending summer vacations either on land or sea depending on whether we had a boat or not, and then that extended to Trey and Chad and their burgeoning families.

You are thinking *Donna, stop!! We cannot keep track of all these kids!* Well, there is no quiz at the end. Just relax and let these details slide by. Two years after the three 2000 babies, Rick and Jenny welcomed a fourth little cutie named Ella and soon after, Dan and Lisa greeted baby Allison.

The sudden growth of our family was breathtaking. Before long, I asked Ken about the possibility of expanding our family room to accommodate our loved ones. In January of 2003 he did just that. I thought my idea simple: a room addition. But my husband, a perfectionist when it comes to his building projects, had other ideas. Before long, he had taken our 35 year old house down to the studs. Indeed, he was going to fulfill my wish. But I had no idea that he was going to build me a brand new house! He even tore off the stucco and put up beautiful wood siding! I think the only objects he left from the original construction were one bathtub and one toilet. Within one year I had a brand new home. It was thrilling and to this day I walk around the rooms in wonderment!

One morning I was standing in front of the new granite fireplace, staring at it. I had spent my young growing-up years in a one-room beach cottage that had belonged to my grandmother. This new house amazed me. Anyway, Ken caught me studying the fireplace and laughed out loud. "Donna, you are too funny! I don't know why this is so surprising to you! You worked your rear off all those years with the rental business. We both did. Before that you often studied all night when you were in school. Are you forgetting you worked part-time to get through college?"

Continuing to admire the granite, I responded thoughtfully, "Kenny, I was used to the 'dig in and get 'er done' aspect of life. Hard work; the struggle. I never translated it into ultimate rewards."

"Love, you are failing to recall our decades of rental horror stories. How we entertained our friends with our wildest tales?"

Laughing now, I replied, "I do remember painting a unit one day after school, and when I turned around Rick had his little head stuck in the rung of a ladder-back chair. He was only two. My sidekick. I had to call the fire department to help free him. That seems funny now."

"Not that funny," added Ken. "I remember how our friends could not believe that the people at eviction court knew you by your first name, or all the abandoned units we had to deal with where the tenants had skipped out; leaving refrigerators full of food; the electricity long since shut off. Or worse. Like the dogs that had been locked in a patio for months without anyone cleaning up!"

"Yikes. Don't remind me!"

"How about that time there was a dead body in an apartment?" Ken reminded me.

"It seems farfetched now, but it wasn't then." I added. "Do you remember my regular Saturday work crew? I gathered up our three youngsters and the neighbor boys and off we went for a day of apartment cleaning and painting."

"I was always so proud of how effective you were with that gang of young workers. I can still see you loading up the blue van: brooms, paint rollers, drop-clothes, and all those children!" Ken paused and looked me in the eye. "Donna you have worked very hard for this."

As he gathered me into a hug, I thought, *really?*

***

The babies continued to come. As our son Rick tells the story, he and his wife Jenny were visiting Chinatown in San Francisco during a summer trip. Inside one of the stores, he found Jenny admiring dolls that resembled newborns. He saw a familiar hunger in her expression as she admired the doll. There must have been a pow-wow, because a few months later during a family Easter party, Rick and Jenny made yet another big announcement: Number Five was on her way! That next winter we welcomed Katie into our now sprawling family.

Once again squeezing in under the wire, as that first decade closed, Dan and Lisa welcomed baby Grace in the summer of 2009. It was my honor and life's great joy to be present at all eleven of those births. For a little girl who had long ago dreamed of being "normal" and having a "normal" adult life, this was bliss; for a girl who met a boy and dreamed about having "a great big family full of energetic little ones," it is hard to find words to express the unparalleled elation I feel.

***

A vivid memory I have is of being at the merry-go-round in Los Angeles' Griffith Park with Ken while we were both college students. I recall leaning back in his arms as he talked about all the kids we would have someday, how we would take them on this merry-go-round. A sweet memory.

As I write this I almost have to pinch myself to believe that all I have described to you came true. I cannot put that kind of joy into words. You might remember from *Cry the Darkness* the story about when I first saw Ken standing at the back door of our friends' house. He was a Boy Scout who had come with his friends to entertain Leanne and me. One look at his clean-cut almost 15 year-old self, and I could not eat nor sleep for the rest of that week. They sang *the love bug bit you and you can't hold still* which was very embarrassing to me because the love bug did *bite* me and never let go. It feels like a gift to still be so in love with my husband.

Anyway, at this writing, all those children are flourishing. We began this summer of my writing with the high school graduations and parties for Jill and Jake. Each of whom were valedictorians of their classes. Their high school careers were outstanding and they have been accepted to top universities. They are hard-working and happy people as are their siblings and cousins. I know that God has blessed me a million fold. The bad part is long in the past and I have worked to use that horrendous education I received at the hands of my father toward good, to help protect women and children, and to savor the precious moments of life.

ONE HUNDRED YEARS OF WEESHA

And so as our immediate family grew, another milestone year was brewing on the Weesha front as 2010 marked the 100th anniversary of our club's existence. By now you know the club likes to celebrate the big anniversaries such as the 75th and even the 90th. For this one we hoped to mark the occasion with an even bigger splash! A planning committee began the preparations and some members wondered if I might write some kind of centennial book as a commemoration. One day it came to me. What if I gathered stories and photos from the current members illustrating what their families were doing 100 years before compared to life today in 2010?

I hope you know me now. Of course I immediately fell in love with this "Then and Now" approach and I set to work to learn more about that time period in American history. Soon my brain was filled with stories about the great fire of San Francisco, the sinking of the Titanic, the first "aeroplane" flight across our continent, water coming to Southern California, the discovery of the North Pole, the orange growers urgent demand for Coolies, the sinking of the Lusitania and unionist bombs blasting the *Los Angeles Times* building. I was rarin' to go!

This time my request for materials was met with great enthusiasm and my email hummed with incoming documents and jpegs. The photos and stories were rich with Americana. One of my favorite photos was a "shocking" one taken in Los Angeles. It was of a member's great aunt. To give you a flavor of what the times were like 100 years ago, she was *driving* a 1909 Kissel car—*imagine a woman driver!* Another favorite was a military photo of the same member's grandfather going off to what was called the Punitive Expedition in World War I, the first U.S. military action using airplanes and trucks.

I was in ecstasy over all these wonderful bits of American history. I dug out photos of my great grandmother standing behind the counter in her pharmacy at 7th and Central in Los Angeles. Janet sent me photos of her great grandparents on their La Habra orange grove. There was a photo of a member's beautiful young grandmother in long-skirted splendor in Puebla, Mexico just before her marriage and immigration to America. The Mexican Revolution made it a good time to come to America.

As I fell to sleep one night I was remembering the Columbian author Gabriel Garcia Marquez and his famous book, *100 Years of Solitude.* He inspired me to call this new book *100 Years of Weesha.* I was excited about the project and dreamed about writing the book.

THE WEESHA CENTENNIAL EVENT

I wish you could have been there. We managed to turn our 100 year anniversary into quite a memorable occasion. I had been asked to lead a sort of history discussion. That got my imagination going and I decided that it would be colorful and fun to become a character from our club's early days. A trip to the costume store helped me to "become" early Weesha pioneer, Josie Berkenstock, a prominent Orange County lady of the 1900's. As part of the festivities we had erected a big top tent. On the afternoon of the history talk, I greeted the audience. This consisted of all the members who cared to share a vivid memory of camp life "back in the day." Since we had invited anyone we could find that ever had anything to do with our club, there was a nice big audience. I began in the persona of Josie and shared one of "my" recollections from 1910:

"Well well, I am so happy to have all of you here in 1910. As you might recall from club lore, I loved to share stories with the children. They would gather around me in front of the old fireplace up at my place. I can still see their eager faces. One of my great talents was my perfection of a mystifying skill. As a smoker of cigarettes I mastered the trick of exhaling so that the smoke appeared to be coming out of my ears!"

"My my, you should have seen the looks on the little ones' faces when I got to that part of the ghost story. Their eyes were as big as saucers. You could hear them thinking, *real smoke is comin' outta her ears!!!!* In those days there was no electricity so you can imagine how dark it was up here and my walls were decorated with buffalo heads and deer trophies. It could be kind of creepy...and if you imagine those big black bears that could be behind every tree...why those children..." Josie laughed at her own scary story.

"Josie" continued like that for a bit which set the mood. Before long the others were sharing favorite memories of feeding watermelon to 50 deer at the front porch, of pulling 100 trout out of the river in a single day, of watching the mule train struggle up the mountain into Big Bear Valley. It was a thrilling afternoon of tall tales but that was just the start of it.

Soon everyone joined in for three-legged races, and country fair style attractions such as face painting and "fishing" for real gold fish. As the sun set, a live western band entertained us as the delicious barbecue was served. Later the dancing began.

Another highlight was a costume parade. Ken surprised me when he dressed up as a 1920's fellow and marched with me as I held up my "Give Women the Vote" sign. I had somehow morphed from being "Josie, the pioneer" to being a suffragette. You can see there was no accountability about staying in character! Everyone was having a lot of fun, especially when Jake showed up as Santa Claus. Lisa was not going to be upstaged by any Santa or Tinkerbelle. She won "most original" with her hat that was a replica of our original stone cabin! No one could believe her creativity on that one. You can imagine that the young ones decorated themselves in boas, tiaras, fairy wings and crazy make-up. We paraded all over the camp to the applause of the others.

The three-day celebration attracted five members of a family who had once owned our cabin. They were little kids when they knew Weesha. As their hosts, we gave them a room where they could rest, and of course they got a tour of their old house. I can still hear them, "Oh look, there's that fireplace screen and even the tools that grandma bought up! It had to be the early 40's." When they got to the old time electric refrigerator with its motor-top now used as a bedroom storage cabinet, we got the whole story of their grandparents bringing it to Weesha only to discover it was too big for the kitchen. It sat for the next 50 years in the living room! When they spotted the claw foot tub and its original rope scratches from its mule train trip up the mountain, they were even more thrilled. All those memories were joyous to me because we had worked hard at historic preservation and this confirmed for me that it had been worth the effort.

A year or so prior to the celebration a devastating fire destroyed a large part of Janet and Paul's wonderful historic home. During the reconstruction, a massive rock was unearthed which we immediately decided had to become a monument. As part of the celebration Ken mounted a brass plaque on it commemorating the anniversary and Paul, as our club president, hosted its unveiling. The entire membership showed up for that and a big toast to one hundred years! It was all very enjoyable. And I topped it off by proudly presenting a hardbound copy of *One Hundred Years of Weesha* to each cabin.

As the tent went down at the end of that weekend and we were folding up tables and chairs, my dear grandson James came over and linked his arm in mine. "Well, Mimi that was some big party." Laughing James remarked, "I think my favorite part was when you and Jake danced. That was wild. I thought Jake was too shy for something like that! Who do you think put him up to it?"

"Ah, I bet there was a cash incentive in there somewhere," I laughed.

"Mimi, so did the party go off like you had hoped?"

"James, it was beyond my wildest expectations! I cannot believe everyone got so into it! The parade was hilarious! Imagine Santa Claus, suffragettes, Tinkerbelle, and cattle rustlers all in the same parade! Hey, didn't I see you carrying around some bags of fish?" I exclaimed.

"I won six goldfish in the fishing booth. That was so cool. I'm taking them home. I hope we do this every year! I know I will always remember this anniversary party!" He concluded with a wide smile.

Memories. I thought. *We are making memories. I still could not believe that our 16 year-old grandson actually danced with me in front of all those spectators! This is too precious.* I smiled again as I folded up the last of the chairs.

CHAPTER FIVE: BRAVING RETIREMENT

"The mind is everything. What you think, you become."
Buddha

July 26, 2012
Avalon Bay, Catalina Island

This morning I went on a power walk all over Avalon. My new hobby and goal was training for the next half marathon. As I walked, I thought back to another July in Catalina, five years before, and a brief encounter with a child that really impacted me. I had almost gotten brave enough to stop teaching, and was determined to turn in my retirement papers in September, when I had an encounter on our annual family Catalina trip that changed things.

I had been out on the swim platform in the harbor when I noticed a wet little boy standing next to me. I saw his young little self, maybe six years old, maybe three feet tall. He was getting ready to swim all the way back to shore, obviously a big challenge. I could see that he was scared. He squared his shoulders and faced the water. He was being brave. He sucked in a big gulp of air and dived off. My eyes filled with tears. My lip quivered. The tears fell down my cheeks. It took less than a second for me to think, *"Oh my gosh!"* as I suddenly saw him fast forwarded ten or twelve years. An entire scene played out in my minds' eye: We were in my classroom. I could see him walking to the podium to give his first speech. He was terrified. He froze. Then I could see him gulp a big breath of air and dive into his presentation.

In that flash of vision I knew that I was not ready to leave my scared-to-death speech students. I made up my mind right then in my wet bathing suit, standing on the swim platform. *No retirement, not now. I cannot do it. I will not leave them!*

It is not entirely clear to me when my teaching career became a passion. It kicked in somewhere down that long road and, the love of it became so strong that as retirement age crept closer, I felt physically ill to even consider it. I worried whether I would be okay without those energetic students every day? Common sense thinking is what teachers give to students, little is mentioned of how much students give to teachers. But I knew. My intuitive inner voice understood that the routine of going to the classroom every single day guided me; helped me to feel whole. However, there was another part of me, the grown up part, that knew it was simply *time*. It had been costing me a bundle in both energy and money to insist upon teaching well past when I had maxed out my retirement income. There were other areas of my life that I wanted to explore; and I simply could not do it *all*. Oh, I had been trying. During a recent spring break, I jumped on an airplane and explored Amsterdam for a week. I gloried in spending an afternoon studying Van Gogh's sunflowers in person, the strokes of his brush, the way he used color.

I was fascinated by the endless canal system, and I was haunted by the visit to Anne Frank's home. I kept thinking about the Monopoly game sitting out in her family's secret hiding place as if she had just stepped away from it. I thought about that 15 year-old-girl being dragged out of her bed, ending up in the gas chamber. That trip was a big experience, showing me and teaching me so much. But two days after my plane landed at LAX, I was right back in the classroom. No getting over jet lag. I was not letting myself recharge. I was not even allowing myself time to process all that I had seen. I needed to think about the details; about that monopoly game, about other similar incidents playing out in our current world, in the Middle East. I had to make some changes, but a big part of me was none too happy about leaving the known path.

Finally, in December 2010 I pulled the plug. I actually turned in my papers. My colleagues were stunned. They assumed that because of my love of teaching, I would still be doing it when my time came to meet my maker. They kept pulling me aside trying to find out the "real" reason why I was retiring; had I developed some terminal disease? I was fine. "You were just chosen 'Teacher of the Year,' you can't quit now!" Yes I could. It was just *time*.

I wanted to go quietly into the good night, but my family insisted we have a gathering to celebrate my forty-five year teaching adventure. I ended up loving the special good-bye celebration. I still see Ken with microphone in hand welcoming my colleagues, our friends and the family. He had somehow managed to assemble all 11 of our grandchildren to the podium in front of the banquet room.

I took my seat and I know a huge grin was plastered across my face. Leanne, my childhood friend, was seated next to me. As Ken began the proceedings Leanne reached over and squeezed my hand. Her husband, Ron, was next to her, Janet and Paul across the table with our other close friends. On this night Jake was the representative for the grandchildren. Ken introduced him and Jake took charge of introducing the grandchildren. Jake moved down the long row of our many kids offering the mike to each of them to introduce themselves.

I marveled at his good looks, his poise and the fact that he was my own flesh and blood. When it was Allison's turn, shyness got the better of her and she could not manage a single sound, Jake stepped in and announced her name. When he finally came to the end of the row, he handed 15 year-old Jill the microphone. In her strong grown up voice she said, "I'm Jill and this is Grace," as she held up the baby.

I could feel a magic in the crowd. For years I had reveled in telling my colleagues about the birth of all these kids. But I suppose it is one thing to hear about someone's family, and quite another to see them dressed up, three in high heels, nearly grown, standing in front of you.

I took a minute to look around the crowd. My friends were riveted by the children. Jaycelin was up next, at 13, tall and graceful. She took the microphone. In her clear feminine voice she began: "Mimi I have written this poem for you. *Mimi, the matriarch, of our clan, she is wise, brave, and we are her biggest fans, forty-five years at Cypress College, what a ball! Boy, you have outlasted them all!*

That line drew laughs as I really was the last one standing of the original faculty who opened the college in 1966. As Jaycelin shared her delightful and original lines, I was spellbound. Every cell attuned to the children, to Jaycelin. She was exquisite. *Already a young woman. It took bravery to address her grandmother, her "Mimi," in front of all these people, yet she was all smiles and shine.* I let myself be pulled into her lines. I breathed, sneaked another quick peek around the room to the 150 people gathered.

I did one of my quick freeze frames and wondered how could life have gotten this sweet? I could not imagine. Here I was surrounded by my happy successful adult children and their spouses, all the grandchildren. Mom was here after a harrowing health scare a few months before, and all of my sisters and two of my brothers, my closest friends, my colleagues and a dozen students. It almost seemed unreal. But it was real. I had created this life. I had. My eyes misted over.

I tuned back to Jaycelin as she concluded. *"We are all so proud of you, but it is now time for Cypress College to bid you adieu. We love you Mimi!"* The audience burst into applause.

Jake had more to say, "Mimi, we all love you so much. You take us on trips. You take us places, ah, same thing." The crowd laughed. "Mimi you are.............." The rest of the evening was a blur of speeches and jokes, some at my expense and lots of eating and dancing. My two good buddies, Patrick and Stuart did a marvelous job as co-emcees and my communication studies colleagues sang to me.

When it was my turn to respond to the tributes and presentations I ran a little skit, donned a velvet crown and purple robe, and with scepter in hand, crowned the next most senior faculty member. And so vested with my imaginary powers, my good buddy and communication colleague, Pat Ganer, became the next "Matriarch of Cypress College." Pat, always a good sport, on bended knee, received the special anointment I was dishing out with my made-up powers and scepter. As I placed the velvet crown on her head more laughter rang out. It was a lot of fun.

Truly, it was a night to remember. It left me humbled in a big way. I could not believe all the love that poured over me and reminded me, once again, how much my Cypress College teaching years had and will always mean to me.

REINVENTING MYSELF

Now was my time. I knew that. But what did that mean? One of my concerns had always been that if I were to stop teaching, I might isolate. I have always been good at playing alone. I love to paint, to write, to read, walk the dogs, to think. I knew I did not want to let myself do that. It would be so easy. But I love being around people too much to allow myself to go there.

On the first weekend of the New Year, 2011, and my new life, two weeks after my retirement party, Ken read aloud an announcement in the *Orange County Register* about a coming presentation entitled "Reinvent Yourself!" It seemed a perfect fit. I signed up online and went to my first meeting. I enjoyed the welcoming group of women and the emcee was a hoot. They called themselves Womansage. It felt comfortable to be in the company of 100 other women, about my age, who were also trying to figure out just what to do with the rest of their lives. I paid my membership fee on the spot and signed up for a year. I felt like I had found a home base.

In the fall leading up to this big life change, I began to say yes to everything. During our Thanksgiving celebration at Julie and Justin's home, Justin's mom, Ann, invited me to go trekking in Nepal the next fall. I said, "Sure." A few weeks later, while I was visiting my sister Sandy, she discovered that I was going to have an open schedule in the spring she said, 'Sis, then you can come to Israel with me!" I said, "Sure." On top of those two commitments our family had already made reservations for a two-week long safari in Africa in July. Clearly I was discovering some wonderful ways to structure my new life, but I wanted more substance than a merry-go-round of constant travel. I wanted to put down roots somehow.

One of the key lessons I have emphasized with my students has always been about living an *intentional* life; that it is important to follow your heart. I was also clear that it was a luxury to live in an industrialized nation which provides a lifestyle leading to increased longevity. It awes me that I get to live at a time when humans live longer than ever before. I was determined to have this "extra" time in my life count.

Across the years when the topic of quitting teaching came up, my colleagues would hear me asking, "Do you really think there is *life* outside of my Humanities Classroom 102?" They laughed at me. They mostly took it as a joke, but I wasn't really kidding. My teaching life simply worked for me, but as you know it was *time*. I felt vigorous, still had "juice" enough to do more. So I began to plan. I created a new mission statement, continued to add to my "goals" book, and began to imagine a new kind of life. I wanted it to be rich with adventure and creative endeavors. And I wanted to continue to work with others sharing what I knew.

SETTING THE CORNERSTONES

(I know, there is only one...)

Cornerstone # 1 – Physical Activity and Making New Friends. I realize now with the distance of two-and-a-half-years what an amazing luxury it was for me to set cornerstones of my new life. Here I was sixty-eight years young, in good health with the security of my teaching retirement income. I was in a position to choose my course. For years as I headed home from my morning dog walk, I would imagine *what if I could just keep walking? What if I did not need to get on the freeway?*

That time had come. Free from the confining commuter schedule, I began to walk longer distances. The dogs and I took to the hills behind our house. My friend invited me to walk with her friends. I enjoyed them and invited them to hike the trails by our mountain house. As the walking continued across the months, we became close friends, celebrating birthdays and holidays together. We named ourselves the Power Walkers.

The culture within our immediate family includes a lot of competitive sports. Julie, for example thinks a rousing 10 mile warm-up run in the morning is invigorating. She and her "Racy Lady" friends frequently get together to climb mountains or enjoy a 15 mile trail race in Big Bear. Dan recently completed the Javalina 100 Miler, while Rick thinks nothing of knocking off a 50 mile course in mountainous Catalina. Both Rick and Dan recently completed the Coeur D'Alene Ironman Triathlon which is a 112 mile bike ride, a full marathon and a 2.5 mile swim. They did that event with relative ease. Ken has completed almost 20 marathons himself. You can see that I live in a very determined family. Ken realized how much my titanium hip and I were enjoying the power walking and so he began a new crusade. "Donna, you aced that 5K at Avalon with all those hills. You easily took first place in your age group, I think you should do the Orange County Half Marathon. You'd love it and it would give you a goal with your walking!"

I thought he had lost his mind. It had been only a few years since I had been hobbling around on a bad hip. The replacement surgery had been a miracle and I was pain-free and limp-free, but completing 13.1 miles all at once? Clearly my husband did not get that when I came in at Avalon I was simply trying not to embarrass myself by coming in last! He is, however, a persuasive guy. Daughter-in-law Jenny jumped on board the half marathon bandwagon and offered, "Donna I will do it with you. I will help pace you."

Julie enthused, "Mom, it will be fun. I will run ahead and finish the course and then come back and speed walk in with you and Jenny. You'll love it. I will help train you!"

So I thought, *well okay then, I will power walk the course. Why not?* Ken immediately signed me up.

And they were right. I did love it and finished with a respectable time. That was the beginning of my competing in half marathons. I admit that I have been enjoying them. My new life also afforded more opportunity to ride my beautiful horse, Pixie. So you see what the answer to that unspoken question is, (What if I could keep on going?) Answer: I will keep going FAR! I love this T.S. Eliot quote: "If you do not go too far, how will you know how far you can go?" It could be that I have embraced that thought in other areas as well.

Cornerstone #2 - Travel. With three big international trips scheduled for the first year of my new life, that cornerstone had pretty much set itself. (I know that there is only one cornerstone when you build a building.......we cannot get too technical here! But ultimately there are four to a building!) I was excited about all three trips and rightly so. The trek and elephant safari in Nepal were some of the most inspiring and amazing adventures of my life. I want to tell you more about that later because you have to know about my "moment" with my new 11,000 pound elephant friend. I also want to tell you a bit about Israel and I am sure you can imagine the thrill of witnessing thousands of wild animals marching across the Serengetti with nine of your family members next to you in the Range Rover. Let's save that for later.

Cornerstone #3 - New Ventures. This aspect of my new life included opening a life coaching practice and offering professional speaking programs. I named my business Your Time Now Communications and hired my sister Diana to help me. She is a genius with website design and electronic technology. With her help my business was soon up and running with a beautiful website, business cards and professional materials. I opened an office and began offering communication workshops. I was invited to join networking groups and made many new contacts. Womansage invited me to sit on their board of directors. I also volunteered to be the life coach for their Transitional Makeover Program. I began to occupy myself by creating adventure PowerPoint programs to share in my grandkids' classrooms. I have also become involved with the Boys and Girls Club. As I write this, a young man whom I coached with his speech when he was competing for Youth of the Year at the local club, has gone on to win, county, state and now regional competition. One more round and the prize includes an audience with the President at the White House. I am thrilled for him. He was just a skinny little boy in first grade with not enough English to even ask where the bathroom was, and he graduated as Valedictorian at his high school. Fantastic! You see I have discovered some very cool stuff to become involved with and I have loved every second of it!

Cornerstone #4 - Family Time. What I have not shared with you is the fact that Dan and Lisa moved in across the street from us over ten years ago while Rick and his family have always lived close by. This has allowed Ken and me the delicious and amazing experience of being surrounded by our grandchildren. We see them frequently and enjoy the comings and goings that proximity offers. With this new life, I am able to see even more of them. To top it off, the last grandchild is still a baby and her adorable self lives across the street! I have the luxury of more time and energy for them.

Around 2008, Ken and I made an intriguing decision. We committed to taking each grandchild on his or her own "eighth grade trip." My role model for this idea was my grandmother, Maymie, who took me on a six week cruise of the South Pacific when I was 19. It was life changing for me and helped me set the goal of wanting to see the world. Maymie was a positive influence in my life. She often was a part of our frequent family trips across America.

Ken and I were captivated by this idea of traveling with the grandchildren. The trigger point happened one ordinary day. We were discussing life and travel after just returning from a trip to China with our daughter, Julie, and her family, when suddenly 12 year-old Jill put her hand on her hip and in a burning tone announced, "I have not *even* been out of the country!" Ken and I looked at each other and kept a straight face, but later in private we could not help but laugh at her indignation! It was not long after that we decided to take her and sister Megan to British Columbia.

A favorite memory from that trip was High Tea at the famous Empress Hotel in Victoria. As we followed the host through the elegant dining room to our table, I was struck by a fond memory of Maymie taking Sandy and me to the same High Tea when we were similar ages as Megan and Jill. My mind's eye could visualize young Sandy and Donna all dressed up, strolling through the same dining room. Hot tears swelled in my eyes. I had to take some deep breaths. It was intense to be reliving something so sweet from my time with my grandmother, to be sharing it with my grand girls. Ken sensed that I was having a strong emotional response. To help change the mood, when his tea was served, he painstakingly lifted his tiny tea cup to his lips and as he did so he stuck out his pinky finger. The girls and I could not help falling into laughter. The last thing my very masculine husband would ever do would be to sip tea, let alone raise his pinky finger. It was too funny and the girls and I could not stop giggling.

That trip proved that at least two of the children were good travelers. The next trip was to New York City and Niagara Falls. We learned that we had phenomenal travelers:

no complaining, no whining, no moods. They were so delightful that I came up with a new idea. I could attempt bigger trips. My initial solo experiment was to take two on a cruise around the Greek Islands, a place I had yet to visit. I invited my daughter's two oldest, Jaycelin, age 12, and Jake, 14. Past trips had been with Ken or the children's parents. This was going to be just me in charge, so to increase the adult ratio I invited my dear friend, Mary, who brought her 11 year-old granddaughter. We thought a party of five of us might be more fun and it was.

I will never forget the breathtaking moment when I looked out of my state room port hole as we sailed into the harbor of Santorini Island, the harbor was the most distinctive I had ever seen, as it is a caldera. After a volcano erupts it collapses creating a chamber, which in this case filled with sea water, making a gigantic circular harbor, big enough for a hundred cruise ships. Seeing where we were, I raced to find the kids, taking two stairs at a time. They had to see this! It was incredible. As I took the last step up to the deck, I spotted Jake and Jaycelin leaning against the railing studying this spectacular sight. It is not every day you sail into what was once clearly the center of a volcano. I could see that they were engaged in an intense conversation. I did not interrupt them, and quietly took a place at the railing. When they stopped talking I went over and stood behind them and put an arm around each, and said nothing. It was too powerful to spoil with words. Later they told me they were realizing that they wanted more travel, that they too wanted to be citizens of the world like I was, their Mimi. Witnessing that exchange between them might not seem like much, but I *knew* I had witnessed a life turning decision on their part. It answered a dream I have for them. I want my grandchildren to feel brave enough to take on the entire planet.

The next year, Jake signed up for a language immersion program and spent two weeks in Argentina, and as I write this Jaycelin has just returned from two weeks in Costa Rica where she planned a summer camp program for kids and then, with other like minded teens, taught the program. Both have improved their Spanish speaking skills, and have a hunger to see more of the world. I could not be happier than I am about this. The next trip on the agenda is an adventure through the Andes of Ecuador and the Amazon River headwaters. This time I will be taking Megan and Jaycelin who will continue to hone their language skills.

So with the infrastructure of my reinvented self in place, I moved forward.

CHAPTER SIX: SHE SAVED HERSELF

"A person can change the future merely by changing his attitude."
Zahid Abus

August 2012
San Juan Capistrano, CA.

As I was mucking out the horse corral this morning I began to shift my focus from my day's energetic 4-mile power walk with my sporty lady friends to this afternoon's more serious business. A message had come in from the city's community services office telling me that five new participants would be attending today's Loss of a Loved One support group for which I am the facilitator. I needed to tamp down the glowy enthusiasm that invariably resulted from being with the power walking ladies. As I shoveled, I reflected on this journey into the world of grief for which I had volunteered. Some might think it an ill fit considering how silly and jumpy I can be, but actually it is some of the most meaningful work I have ever done.

I remembered my deep frustration when I was at my lowest point, when I felt like I was drowning in grief over the whole mess of having to intervene against my father. I had scoured the book stores looking for help; all I found was a lame book of poetry; no help at all. In the back of my mind I made a promise that if I were ever in the position of helping others with their grief, I would offer them coping strategies, actual action steps toward feeling better. At the time, I did not have any idea about the how of it, but for sure I knew that I "got it" about the treachery and agony of the grief- strewn road; what a nightmare of inconsolable despair and actual physical pain it gives those who stagger along its many mean turns. I thought more about it and realized that, in many ways, grief's ugly head had shown up with many of my students across the teaching years.

A poignant memory flooded my thoughts. It was of a forty-something woman student I had in class about five years ago. She was a mother of two who had lost custody of her daughters. She was enrolled in my Interpersonal Relationship class. I thought about her, about her grief. With those thoughts, I recalled the last meeting of the class and the closing assignment. I was running a simulation experience. The goal was for the students to begin to consider intentionality and goal setting in terms of their life direction. Each student was required to come "as the person they wanted to be in 10 years." They were to dress the part and role-play the details of their future life. The role-play activity was a favorite and utilized the creative right hemisphere of their brains. Students all across campus talked about it. It was a thrill to facilitate; to see their imaginative ideas. On this particular day we had a two hour block of time for our "class reunion" and its pot luck luncheon.

We had reserved a big area on the balcony level of the gym which had previously been a student center. It was festive in itself with ping pong tables and arcade games lining the walls. On this day, when I opened the double wide doors I was welcomed by the dozens of helium balloons hanging down from the ceiling, and soft rock music welcoming us, I broke into happy laughter. There was even a huge sign announcing, "Reunion Class of 2008." The decoration committee had out done itself. The room felt charged with electricity. I thought to myself *and they wonder why I keep teaching, why I love my work? These students are just too much fun!* I thought of that oft given advice, *if you choose work you love, you will never work a day in your life!* So true, so true!

I, of course, came dressed as a future self. This day I was wearing a silk robe from China with a bejeweled headdress adorning my head. My "role" was travel writer. I began to mingle, greeting and shaking hands with all these "former" students. As I approached one young man dressed in surgical scrubs, I began with one of my standard corny lines, "Wow, so aren't you Jeff? Why you have not aged a day. You almost look the same as you did way back when you were in my class." My silliness got a laugh.

"Well hi. Yes," responded Jeff picking up our fantasy game. "You remember, Jeff from the back row. I'm glad to be here. I had to fly in from Florida. Got in late last night. Some delays. Air traffic control stuff."

"So tell me." I continued, "I cannot help but notice that there is a live snake wrapped around your neck! It's not a python I hope?"

"No, the python's back at the office." He joshed back, eyes sparkling in merriment.

"So spill, what's this about? Are you a mad scientist or what?" I asked.

"Duh. Don't you remember? I was all about vet school. My passion is animals? I have a private practice in Florida. My specialty is exotic animals."

"Well I'm very impressed. Hey, isn't that Melanie over there? Remember her?" With that I ambled off to meet up and become "reacquainted" with the others, after all, it had been "ten years."

As I chatted with the next iterations of Tiger Woods, three guys huddled in the corner, I scanned the big room. I noticed a woman in a long white dress standing apart. I watched her for a minute as each of these "Tiger Woods" guys showed off his golf clubs and pastel shirt. I took a deep breath and exhaled slowly. This was hugely fun. The entire class was so in the moment. One young woman came up to me and proudly showed me her "wedding" photos complete with names and details of her make-believe wedding! The fantasy continued, I turned around and a student, Kelly, grabbed me in a bear hug. "Dr. Friess, I've missed you!" Her eyes were alive with fun. "So hey, do you remember me?"

"Of course I do!" I responded picking up her line, "I remember, let me think now…. you sat behind Paul who was taking his band on the road to Australia. Weren't you going to study police science?" I added, pulling in some actual details about her. She beamed her reply as she flashed the fake gold FBI badge affixed to her belt buckle. I examined her more closely; she was in full FBI garb down to the dark glasses and earpiece!

The "reunion" continued like that through lunch. There were about 45 people as some students had brought friends or a parent. During it all I kept my eye on the lady in white satin. I had not yet made it over to chat with her.

For the grand finale we stood around in a big circle and shared a short update of who we were and what we were doing here in "2018." Around the circle we went, when it was Lola of the white satin's turn, she said, "This is my coffin dress. I am dead."

Everyone froze. There was a stunned silence. I tried to move the group back to the "reunion" tempo but it was hard with her shocking declaration. Somehow we managed to finish up the activity and bid goodbye for the summer. Later, after the clean up, a few of us lingered around to talk to her. She was forthcoming. "I have been drinking so much that my liver function is failing." Her voice dropped to a rough whisper, I could smell alcohol on her breath. "I have bloody stool. The doctor says I don't have much time. I will be gone in a year."

After the others left, she shared more with me. I listened carefully. "That court hearing is over. I lost custody of my girls. My ex got me for the drinking. It is hopeless."

I could feel her despair and see the grief etched deeply into her pretty face. I heard her out. She cried. After commiserating with her about her girls, I challenged her, "Lola, this is stupid. You are a young woman. Stop drinking. Stop it! This is so not fair to your girls. You can do this. Stop drinking. You do not have to die." *Surely she had been told this before!*

I will never forget the oddest expression that crossed her face as I said that. It was almost like she had not thought of other options. After a bit, with dry eyes, she hugged me good-bye and that was it, the end of the semester and a three-month-long summer break.

A year or more later, I had just excused my class when I looked up to see her standing in the doorway to my classroom. She was all smiles, "Dr. Friess, I did it." This was out of context for me and I didn't know exactly what she was talking about. She looked good, she looked sober. "I stopped drinking. My liver has recovered. I get my kids every weekend." She stopped and grinned at me. "Dr. Friess you saved my life!"

I knew that I had not saved her life. She had saved her own life, but Lola is but one of many such cases I encountered over my career. There were beautiful eighteen-year-old young women whose mothers had died of cancer and young men struck down by bullets, forced to learn to live life from a wheelchair. I realized that I had been partially emerged in grief-work for decades. I had learned that sometimes all it takes is telling a person that they can change, that it is possible, and they do it. To me the power of permission is extraordinary. I was describing this phenomenon about Lola and the coffin dress to my psychologist friend, Liz, saying it is so "crazy" that people ascribe so much power to others (to me is what I meant in this case). She said, "It is not crazy at all. You were already installed as an inspirational person for her, so it's just like a guru telling her exactly what she's known in her heart for a long time. And kudos to you for the clear (and I'm very sure, kind) intervention."

I wasn't sure how kind I had been, but I am certain that I was *very* clear and very direct.

***

As I put away the wheelbarrow and headed up to the house to get ready for my Loss of a Loved One group, I remembered when it occurred me that I could do this kind of work. It was the first month of my new life. I had just retired from Cypress College. On this particular rainy January day in 2011, I finished up a community talk entitled, "Refresh Yourself" which included strategies for feeling better in the new year. There were about 50 very receptive people in my audience. As I packed up my gear and headed for my car, three ladies followed me, filled with questions about coping with their recent personal losses. Two were new widows and one was newly divorced. We stood by the trunk of my car for some time. I listened carefully as they explained how desperate they felt, how bereft. They needed some answers. It seemed like they had no idea what to do with their grief. I continued to listen as I stood there in the grey day. When they finished, I shared my best thinking with them. It was a first step down another challenging path.

111

During the forty-five minute commute home, I pondered their questions and thought more about them. I recalled my own agony and how little help there had available for me when I needed it.

Suddenly a thought occurred to me. What if *I* could offer a Loss of a Loved One support group in my own community? If I offered such a group there would be more than support. I would teach tools to help ease the pain.

That evening excited words tumbled out of my mouth as I shared my idea with Ken. I wanted to facilitate an official, free, support group through the city. As a veteran former councilman he knew his way around city hall. He told me how to go about it. Within a month I had approval, was finger printed and the work began.

I am often asked, "How can you do it?" People want to know how I can listen to all that pain without it affecting me?
I can listen. It does affect me, but not in a negative way. I think helping others is helping me and I am drawn to this. I think a lot about the wonderful heartbroken people I have gotten to know. I see how courageous they are, moving forward even though they have holes in their hearts. It is my privilege to work with them, to have their trust at such a vulnerable time, to hold them in my heart. I cannot imagine not offering it.

I have seen first-hand the positive results when devastated people are taught what to expect and to understand that grief has stages and that it is a long and jagged journey; when they learn that it is normal to feel overwhelmed, that they are not crazy, I see relief in them. Certainly there is no magic bullet to remove the pain, but through personal understanding and being in the presence of supportive others, where it is safe to cry, seems to bring comfort. The fact that they get to talk about what they are feeling and to be heard is a big part of it.

The members of our group frequently lament that their friends have fallen away, or are impatient with them to "be over it." One lady told us that her friend actually voiced these words, "you should be over this by now." Her husband had only been dead for a few months! Like there was a time limit on grief.

I also teach that they *themselves* must do the grief work and it may take a very long time. For the widows who were married for 67 years and for the parents who have lost a child, we talk about the fact that they will probably never "get over it," but they will somehow learn to live with the loss. I share hope. It is possible to feel better but it takes some baby steps toward a change and a whole lot of courage.

For years I have studied the research on Resiliency; human hardiness. I teach about Initiative as a trait that breeds strength. I encourage my participants to find something they feel passionate about and dig into it. I knew from my years in therapy that having seriously pursued the art of portraiture helped me cope with the stress surrounding my father and my childhood.

In group we develop action plans and accomplish a few life changes. One of the wonderful widows in our group, who lost her beloved husband after 65 years, took our advice. At Christmas time last year she took off and visited Cuba! She amazed us all. Even with her broken heart, she moves forward and celebrates life. She inspires us all.

When we talk about change it is with the idea that making a change can help. It does not matter how big or small. It does not have to be a sojourn to Cuba. It could be something like making a new friend, getting out of the house once a week, losing a few pounds, organizing the pantry, helping a family member, joining a class, or volunteering. All I know is that whatever it is we are doing, I see a great deal of healing and as the months pass, a whole lot of smiling. One lady often says to the group, "I know it sounds crazy but I really look forward to grief group." Of course it is not crazy. It is all about support and feeling safe.

Since I have begun my love affair with the new findings in neuroscience, I have been teaching about the brain's "narrative." It is something like a film reel that spools thoughts around and around in one's head. By taking responsibility for one's feelings, it is possible to take *action* steps toward feeling better. It is possible to reappraise, that is *reframe*, a situation. It allows one to take control over one's brain.

Negative thoughts can feel overwhelming but we can work to lessen them. Scientists are concluding that it is possible to "train" the brain to get back on track and stop the negative story that dwells in one's head. The bereaved often complain that they feel "stuck." This brain information can help to free them from that negative "film reel" and help them to stay focused on the present. I will tell you more about this later.

The support group participants are diverse in all aspects, including their losses. Most have lost a spouse, a parent, or a child, to death; some to divorce. Others have lost their health or their career. They begin by sharing their feelings of fear, anxiety and sadness. One lady arrived in our group and simply stated, "I do not know how to do this," meaning she did not know how to grieve the fact that her 28 year-old daughter had only a few more weeks to live. As a unit, we in the group understood. There is empathy and sharing. I worked to guide her to focus on the time she had left with her daughter, and to force herself to stop obsessing on what she would do after her daughter passed away, to stay in the present. She and I are still in contact. Her daughter did die, but the mother seems more at peace with it. There are so many stories like that.

Another woman lost her husband and both parents within a few months. She was devastated, but she kept coming. Before too many months, the keening had stopped, she got better. At this writing she is a top saleswoman for her real estate business. She is moving forward and I can see that the group makes a difference. The members have become friends and see each other outside of our meetings. There is even "Movie Wednesday" for some of the recent widows.

I know they are feeling better and this is something that I can do to help in the world. My little words here on the paper seem limp compared to how powerful it is for me to be a part of their process. I care deeply about them.

CHAPTER SEVEN: WHALE OF A TALE

"Some things you learn in calm and some things in a storm."
Huffington Post

July 25, 2012
Family Vacation
Catalina Ferry

On this beautiful day I awoke just after 4 a.m., a recent unwelcome habit; however this was wakefulness out of excitement, not crippling anxiety. I'd been having a hard time lately. We headed to Catalina Island, for our family's favorite vacation. All of our kids and all our grands would be there as well as my brother Chad's family. The day started well. Ken and I fed our many animals and headed to the harbor with Allie and Lauren to make the channel crossing on the Catalina Express, the ferry to the island.

We were about twenty minutes into the crossing when the captain came over the loud speaker shouting, "Blue whales. There it is! The blow! We are going whale watching!" Within minutes he had gone off course, stopped the engines, and opened the bow to us. Lauren, Allie and I quickly scooted forward. With each child securely tucked under my arms, we sat excitedly on a bench in the very front. As we settled into our seats we heard a gasp come from the other passengers on the bow. We looked around and there it was, a distant blow. Then another, we strained our eyes and before long we witnessed more blows and glimpses of the sleek black back of a mighty blue whale! The captain came on again, "He has gone down. He will be up in five minutes. Hold on! Everyone sit down!"

Ken slid in next to me. We scanned the horizon for any sign of the whale. We held our breath. I could feel the electric current of energy throbbing between myself and the girls. Soon there was another blow, closer now, and then a sight which was only of my dreams. I heard the man next to me whisper to his son, "Those Blues have a 5000 liter blow capacity!" I could hardly believe what I was witnessing.

The crowd waited. Suddenly a glorious shiny black whale tail broke through the surface of the blue water! The crowd exclaimed in unison and then fell silent. The whale gave us a glorious extended show of his magnificent 36 foot long tail fluke. The tail and time seemed to stand still. What a beautiful long perfect moment. After the tail slipped silently below the surface we dared to breathe. The silence on the bow continued for a long magical moment! Some would say we had shared a God moment. I had been boating all my life, since childhood and never had I witnessed such a breathtaking and dazzling sight. I knew I would never forget it.

The captain called us back to our seats and the bow was again closed. Before long, the rhythmic rocking of the ferry and its roaring engines soon lulled us into relaxation. Allie at nine was getting sleepy. She came into my lap. I gently stroked her perfect pink cheek, remembering comforting my own children that way. Allie's weight felt like a gift in my arms. I closed my eyes and rested my chin on her blonde curls, the fear gripping my soul abated for the moment. For the next 40 minutes, with closed eyes, I kept my thoughts on the majesty of the whale as I basked in the peaceful glory of holding this sleeping child. I thought *they are all growing up so fast.* I knew not to miss a single minute of it.

I thought of the end-of-life book by Eugene O'Kelly, I had just finished. At age 52, Mr. O'Kelly discovered he had but six weeks to live. During those last weeks he came to understand some life lessons that he had missed prior to his diagnosis of terminal brain cancer. He wrote a book about them. His book is a warning about how important it is to stop along life's journey to collect precious moments. He confessed in his wonderful book, *Chasing Daylight: How My Forthcoming Death Transformed My Life,* that at the end, in those last few weeks, he had collected more precious moments than during the previous 52 years! I thought about his harsh lesson: *we do not have time to live agonizing in anxiety, fear or rage.* I got that, but it was hard to keep my anxiety at bay.

***

Ten days earlier, Saturday July 15th became a time dividing day for me and not in a good way. I awoke to discover that I could not see out of my strong right eye. Ken was reading the paper as I came out into the family room. The world looked blurry through my right eye. *Surely it is just foggy from sleeping...*

"Honey. Ken. The vision out of my right eye is not right. It is blurry."

I kept my cool but to say that I was alarmed by this sudden turn of events would be an understatement. Ken came over to me. He examined my eye. After more than an hour, it still had not cleared up. We were both worried. We talked about it. We hoped, maybe, somehow, it was a cataract or something that could be fixed.

I put in a phone message to our optometrist friend. We tried to remain calm. I poured a cup of coffee. I was still hoping the vision would clear up. We talked about it, but neither of us had any idea what was going on with it. To go from 20/20 to practically nothing was frightening. It was like looking through a very thick white lace curtain. I could see a bit of color and some clarity scattered amidst the fog. By early evening our friend got back to me. I explained in detail what had occurred.

Her concerned voice asked, "Donna, look straight ahead. Is your peripheral vision still in tact?"

"Yes, that has not changed all day. It has been the same blurry way all day."

She was relieved with my report. Apparently my eye was not deteriorating. I did not have to go to the hospital. We made arrangements for me to come into the office first thing Monday morning for an evaluation. I thanked her and hung up. I guessed that was the good news. My injured eye was not becoming more blind, at least not for the moment...

Somehow I got through Sunday. I had scheduled a professional photo shoot with my horses for that day. I kept my appointment. The photographer pointed his camera and I smiled on cue. Certainly, I am very accomplished at stuffing bad things into the corners of my mind. The photographs with the horses came out beautifully. Perhaps being in their corral and caressing them comforted me. For a brief interlude I forgot about the terror of the blindness, but in the close-up head shots anyone who knows me can see that the light within my soul was diminished.

Monday morning Ken and I went to the eye specialist for a medical evaluation. By the end of the day I had been sent to a retinal specialist. Alarmed by this change in my health, Julie drove up from San Diego and took over chauffeuring me to the retinal specialist. After dilating my eyes and many more tests, the doctor gave us the results. Julie took careful notes. The diagnosis was an occlusion in the central retinal vein with bleeding which was affecting the macula. I had 20/500 vision in that eye.

"Doctor," asked Julie, "what about the vision in my mom's left eye? Will that eye be okay?"

The doctor flashed a reassuring smile. "Why she has a 75% possibility of keeping it!" He enthused.

What? I might lose my left eye's vision as well? That thought had never occurred to me. I immediately began to problem-solve. What would I do if I went completely blind? A thought which, at that moment, seemed entirely possible. My brain raced with solutions. I thought of how many times I had warned my clients and even my family members, "We have to do what we want to do *now* as we do not know what lies in the future. Anything can happen." I realized that I truly believed that but I meant *anything can happen to others, not to me!*

The competent young doctor explained about the flooding of the macula, about the rods and cones not being able to communicate with each other. That there was a chance to get them to "talk" to each other again and restore some of my vision; that there was a medical procedure. I promptly agreed to his suggestion. He administered a shot directly into my eyeball and signed me up for another shot in a month. He warned, "We have had good results with this, but it is brand new, an off- label use of the medicine, normally used as a chemo treatment for pancreatic cancer. Do not look this up on the Internet!" he warned. "The Internet is not up-to-date with this new protocol. It will only scare you. This may take a year, maybe more, but hopefully some of your vision will be restored."

In the months following the vision loss, my fears and sleeplessness continued. I religiously went for the eyeball shots as I kept up with my commitments; to my clients, my life coaching classes, my professional speaking, and my board of directors work. Life went on as usual, but my anxiety levels were escalating, not diminishing. I feared I was losing control.

As a student of the relatively new academic field of Social Cognitive Neuroscience which became an official discipline in 2007, I had been devouring books on how the brain works for the past two years. I was fascinated by the findings from functional MRI studies and PET scans. This information was allowing scientists to move light years ahead in understanding how the brain works. One concept that particularly resonates with me is the idea that it is possible for us humans to "train our brains." Scientists have discovered that each day we grow new neurons; that it *really may be* possible to teach old dogs new tricks. I was excited about what that could mean for my clients, for depressives, for those haunted by anxiety, for my grief group. If we could learn to more fully control our thoughts we could feel better.

While I shared what I learned, I remained clear that this calming the mind idea was not new in the history of humanity. The ancient philosophies such as Buddhism, had practices for clearing the "chatter" of the brain for some 2000 years.

Through my travels to the Buddhist temples, (one in Katmandu and others across South East Asia,) I learned some important concepts regarding the Buddha. He was born a prince in 566 B.C. and struggled against his own tendencies toward self indulgence, laziness, and negativity. Determined to not let the "bad" side of his personality dominate his life, he devoted himself to discovering a pathway away from suffering and toward happiness. He came to understand that one could control one's mind; one could become "mindful." This is an awareness of one's thoughts, words, and actions. He learned to meditate and he developed rules for living in peace and moving toward enlightenment. The Buddhists believe in an afterlife, that there are more lives to come.

Our travel guide, Ole, a Buddhist himself, suggested that perhaps this life view difference between Westerners and Buddhists explains why the Buddhists are known for their peaceful outlook on life. He wondered if Westerners might feel an urgent need to "get it all done" in one lifetime. It was an interesting thought, but I knew that with my anxiety levels increasing, it was indeed time to take action to train my own brain and somehow calm my fears.

I kept up my studies. The cognitive scientists such as Dr. Larry Cahill of UCI and authors including David Rock, *The Mind at Work,* report on some of the newest discoveries in neuroscience. As I told you earlier, they teach that our brain runs a kind of default narrative. Have you ever been "lost in thought?" It was probably that default narrative function. The narrative mode, which seems to run a kind of story in our minds, may be harmless until one has a real problem, and then it can run amok. Telling us over and over that *"it's too hard, they will not like me, I could never land a job like that..."*

David Rock observes that our brain is hard to control but wants to *be in control*, that when our emotions take over, the limbic system is activated, including the amygdalae which are the areas in the brain that ready us in a fraction of an instant to flee or fight! When this part of the brain is activated, the prefrontal cortex, our rational and calm decision maker, goes missing. Researchers believe we have deeply-rooted neural maps within our brains, that make it easy for worry and anxiety to take over. Certainly, as a child of trauma, I have imbedded neural maps for anxiety and hypervigilance. Anxiety might be thought of as the brain preparing to defend against danger, but not actually having a specific way to relieve the stressors.

The amygdalae, two little kidney-shaped areas in our brain, are always on alert to keep us safe. Sometimes people refer to them as the primitive part of the brain. They are wired for survival. When a stressor shows up and there is no action to take, anxiety builds. I knew there was nothing more I could do about my vision. I had to wait and see, and try to live normally. I had followed through with a new internist who put me through an extensive battery of lab tests to ensure that all my systems were healthy.

I was trying, but during the night I would wake up in a panic. I practiced what I had learned. I forced myself to be mentally in the present. I worked to force myself out of the recurring narrative of what ifs: *What if I go completely blind? What will I do? I won't be able to take my dogs on their morning walks. What if I cannot see the smiles on my beautiful grandchildren's faces? What if this is the end of my travel, my driving...my independence....?*

So I concentrated on focusing on the present. I paced my breathing with my sleeping dog, Casey's, deep slow breaths. It helped. It got me out of being scared and back to sleep. That worked until September 9th when Casey suddenly died of heart failure.

So now I had a devastating vision loss and the grief over my beloved handsome boy Casey. It was awful. I cried and I hate crying! I walked and I cried. I could not talk about it. Ken offered to take me to adopt a puppy. He was hoping to comfort me. I knew a puppy would add to my stress, not relieve it. During those weeks I realized that what I was feeling, this deep sense of loss, was a clear reminder of the pain my clients suffered. (Do you see it? Right there! It is my glass is half-full approach to life. I just cannot help myself, can I?)

I kept up my brain science studies. I practiced what I learned: that we cannot squelch an emotion, that we need to acknowledge its power and let the strong feeling pass though. I learned to activate a different part of the brain, for example the motor area. When the gruesome tentacles of the toxic anxiety sneaked out to get me, I got up. I moved around. When I had an anxiety attack in the middle of the night, I would read a book, eat a snack, or water the plants. During the daytime I began to take even more walks, vacuum the house or wrestle with the dogs. The movement activated my motor cortex and the anxiety subsided for the moment. So I worked hard at practicing what I tell my clients; to marinate our brains in our blessings, that *motion is lotion*. My blessings were many; after all, I was not yet blind. And I knew that I had been lucky to have nine years with my beloved dog.

***

Life continued and I followed through with the travel plans I had made for October. I was traveling alone for the first time with a small adventure tour group. Perhaps my eye would heal. The change of scenery might help me to feel better. I visited Southeast Asia: Thailand, Cambodia, Laos, and Viet Nam. The trip was rich with history.

One particularly thrilling day our group awoke at 4 a.m. to give alms to the dozens of Buddhist monks who silently strode by us in the darkness of early morning to collect their food for the day. It was a fascinating experience and one I shall savor for a long time. I laugh when I think about how rattled our group of almsgivers became when we missed a bucket and dropped portions of sticky rice on the ground, or how clumsy we felt trying to get the rice rounded into the proper little balls. There was so much activity on the tour that I easily forgot about my eye and my sadness over Casey.

The three week long trip included several days of speeding up the Mekong River. I loved the fragrant smells of the flowering plants and the feel of the water spray on my face as I stood at the bow of our motor boat. Everything we learned fascinated me. There unfortunately was a dark side to what we were learning as well. We visited the Killing Fields where Pol Pot, the evil dictator who led the Khmer Rouge during the 1970's carried out the genocide of 1.5 million innocent Cambodians. It was gruesome to know what had so recently happened on our planet. A common sight in the villages was to see people missing limbs, the result of the millions of live land mines that are still buried in the nearby fields across much of Southeast Asia. I also climbed deep into the Chu Chi Tunnels of Viet Nam where the Viet Cong hid below our American military bases, coming out under the cover of dark to kill Americans soldiers. Over 58,000 young men from my generation lost their lives on that soil. To what purpose? I am not sure.

I am unable to reconcile the fact of millions who were exterminated by their fellow humans during my lifetime: Germany, Poland, Cambodia, Bosnia and Rwanda, to name a few, with the fact that our species is talented enough and brave enough to walk on the moon and to explore Mars. That we cannot stop genocide, was more than my brain could process. As I tried to make sense of this, I stopped thinking about myself.

I was glad I had taken the trip. I enjoyed rooming by myself. It was a valuable expedition. However, on the long plane ride home I sat next to a young musician who suddenly became ill. By the end of the 20 hour flight, I too was gravely ill. Ken picked me up from the airport and got me home. Two days later, I was still feeling weak, but I had a speaking commitment that I could not break. I rose to the challenge, but within two weeks the illness gave way to vertigo.

One of Ken's associates heard about my rough bout with vertigo; the wheel chair, the rushing to the emergency room; the crippling dizziness, and she called me. She had suffered with vertigo for years and was a walking encyclopedia about it. She was very reassuring. She thought I might have picked up a virus on my travels and it had somehow affected my inner ear. She shared her experiences and began to put me at ease. I felt safe with her and admitted how much trouble I had been having with anxiety, about my worries over my vision. In her experience, anxiety often accompanied vertigo.

We talked for a long time. I think admitting it out loud somehow let me release some of it. I began to study methods to cope with anxiety. I gobbled up the information and ever since then I have been mostly free of it. I was surprised at the power of simply labeling something and admitting it out loud. Of course I have kept up the regime I learned about training my brain and taking control away from that scary default narrative that my brain wants to run.

In addition, I kept one of my favorite formulas in the front of my mind. Success guru Jack Canfield tells about this technique in his books: $E + R = O$. What this means is, take the **Event**, then *choose* your **Response** to it, and that will determine its **Outcome**. In other words, it reminds us that we have choices. How we choose to respond to events determines how they will affect us. It is a "train your brain" technique.

Here, in a nutshell, is some of what I learned:

COPING WITH ANXIETY
- Admit to feeling anxious. Decide to get control of it.

- Stop alcohol and limit caffeine. Take up something that is meditative for you: walking, yoga, reflection. Work to calm your mind.
- Take nice deep breaths. Inhale slowly and exhale slowly for one minute. This can trick your brain into thinking you are calm and it may help you feel calm.
- When you start to obsess or worry, snap a rubber band that is around your wrist.
- Understand that you can make things happen. Anxiety is an old neural pattern deep within our brains. We have used it for a long time. We can retrain our brains.
- Take responsibility for your entire life. Stop any "blame games."
- Spend time around well evolved people, work to avoid Toxic People.
- Figure out your life purpose and stick with it. Live through your purpose.
- Science has proven that personal growth affects your brain in a positive way.
- Surround yourself with happy positive people.
- Work to help others to grow. Helping others makes us feel better.

***

A year later as this book goes to publication, the eye has improved. Since that awful morning when I awoke to the darkness in my right eye, I have submitted to eyeball shots. Each month they dilate my eye and look around. It is better. It has gone from 20/500 to 20/25, though there is little color to be seen, and it is still like looking through a screen. This improvement is enough that I no longer have the anxiety about future blindness.

CHAPTER EIGHT: THOUGHTS ABOUT HAPPINESS

"Happiness is a choice."
Donna's slogan

Fall 2012

By now you know how worried I was about being able to create a new life direction. A cornerstone to my change was starting the life coaching practice I told you about. Various groups and county agencies began to hire me to put on workshops for their employees while I volunteered for others. One such group included middle class women in mid-life who identified themselves as needing help with serious life transitions. They had signed up for a free ten-week program and my segment included four weeks of life coaching. I recall the first meeting of this new group. It was a lovely spring evening and the thirteen participants were gathered around a large conference table. They did not know each other and the anxiety level in the room was palpable. We began with introductions and as each woman presented her situation, the others listened. There were tears. These were truly hard stories: breast cancer, sudden unemployment, devastating economic loss, homelessness, loved ones who had left or died.

When it was my turn, I acknowledged their pain and then I asked, "Ladies if you were to sum up what you hope to gain from our program here, from the life coaching module I will be presenting, what would it be?" There was a thoughtful silence and then the hands went up. "I need confidence. I feel hopeless," "Well, I feel stuck, I do not know where to turn," "I feel obsolete." And the responses continued.

I took my time and looked at each participant, in a low but intense tone, I queried, "So who at this table has her health?" All the hands went up. I could not believe it. I shared about the recent personal loss our family suffered when our beautiful sixty-two year old friend lost her long battle to cancer. The room grew more silent as the idea resonated within the women: *yes I have my health!*

I took out my oversized hour glass and held it up as I explained that the sand on the bottom represents the past over which we have no influence–it is over; the sand on top symbolizes the future where we do have some influence, but it is the future, it has yet to arrive. Then I pointed out the grains of sand as they passed through from top to bottom. They represent the immediate moment. We have NOW. They looked at me with wide eyes. I felt a seismic shift in the room. Slowly smiles began to replace tears. I could actually feel the change in energy as the participants began to **reframe** their lives. They began to focus on all that they did have. My neuroscience guys would tell us that our thoughts profoundly affect our bodies. As positive thoughts replaced negative ones, my bet is that each woman's brain began to release some of the uplifting hormones such as oxytocin and dopamine.

By the end of the two hour session, a visible change had taken place within the group. I gave them homework, including serious work in writing down all that was "right" in their world. I asked them to actually count up their blessings. For the conclusion to the session, I asked each participant to identify and state out loud, "what is profoundly right with you?"

When our class met the next Tuesday evening, I could hardly believe they were the same women. They were hugging each other hello and joking around. Hope seemed to have replaced despair.

At the end of the 10-week program, we held a graduation ceremony and I thrilled at their individual successes. They had all moved forward toward a better future; some had new jobs, some new living situations, all had a more positive outlook and they were forthcoming with their appreciation to me and to our program director. It was clear to me that under the right circumstances, people can choose to be happier. I also knew that being in a group and sharing themselves with others, making important personal connections, had been part of the positive outcome. Many of the groups I have worked with continue to meet long after the program has ended because the friendships themselves help to uplift them.

It is important to remember that we can significantly affect our own lives by choosing positive responses to difficult situations. In the early 1980's, I had the great privilege of studying with Dr. William Glasser, Father of Reality Therapy. As a student in his class, he reinforced my deeply held belief in the importance of one's attitude. He would say, "We choose everything we do, including the misery we feel." He believed that others can neither make us miserable nor make us happy. It is up to us. He taught that we are much more in control of our lives than we realize. I took his principles to heart. They have been foundational in my own teaching.

CHOOSING HAPPINESS

Recently, I attended a memorial service for my former Division Dean. He had been a good friend and I was sorry he had died. Many of my former colleagues were in attendance. One of my fellow teacher's husbands came up and greeted me. As he hugged me he said, "Donna I still have the saying you handed out at your retirement party. "Happiness is a choice." I have taken that to heart. I put it on the refrigerator and think about it every day. It has been a big help." I smiled and thanked him. Soon all of us congregants took our seats. It was a beautiful service with many tributes to our fallen friend. As I listened to the details of his life and his positive impact on others; how his daughter commemorated him for being present at every single important event in her life, I thought of journalist Anna Quindlen's famous quote: *Just show up!* My friend had done that and much more. He had built a meaningful life. I thought more about happiness and what it takes to achieve it. I recalled a conversation I had with one of my long-time friends, Robin, over lunch the year before.

As we settled into our booth at our meeting point, the Acapulco Restaurant, I remarked, "Robin, do you realize that this September is the 55th anniversary of when we met in junior high school?" I laughed. "I spotted you in homeroom. I knew then I wanted to be your friend."

"Donna, I cannot believe you always remember that homeroom. Can you believe that it has been so long? In so many ways it seems like yesterday, yet we have lived whole lives." Robin replied.

"Robin, you know I have started to write the sequel to Cry the Darkness. It begins with the months after the trial; with the cover story in the <u>Los Angeles Times Magazine</u>. When I started writing, I guess I thought I had to go back through some of that gross stuff, but now I realize that is the past. My work and my writing need to emphasize the "now" not the past. I have been thinking a lot about human happiness and moving forward," I said.

"Donna, I know you are trying to answer how you or others who have been devastated can come back from it. The problem I see is that this is just you! I think your book should have a footprint on the cover. I think what we see in you is just who you are; who you were at birth. Even as kids, don't you remember those years and years of playing jacks and giggling? Don't you remember that lady, Babe, down the street, every time she walked by us she would put her finger across her lips like she was giggling and we would be sent into spasms of hilarity? Don't you remember? We would double over in joyous laughing. You always found the bright note in life. Donna, I know you are all about "happiness is a choice" but I think it is just in you that you keep choosing happiness."

"I saw it raising my children," Robin continued. *"They simply are who they are. Look at me and my sister, we are entirely different. I think this is about you!"* For emphasis Robin looked me square in the eye. Maybe she was thinking that for some people they simply cannot achieve much true happiness.

"Robin, I think there is more to it than that. I can see it with my clients. With the least little nudge I see some of them taking giant steps and becoming unstuck, choosing happiness. One of my beautiful clients has been devoured by grief for five years, and somehow she believed me that she could be happy. I reframed her loss for her; pointed out all the blessings she had enjoyed with her loved one. I watched her. She chose happy. You should see her. She is like a school girl with a new life. She even looked up an old friend from high school and is going to visit him. Robin, this was a lady who had been crying for five years!"

The waitress came to welcome us and the subject changed, but it gave me something to think about. And I have thought about it a lot. You know I believe that happiness is a choice, but for some people it is just easier to be unhappy. That is so sad.

My awareness shifted back to the memorial service, but the concept of what factors allow for happiness continued to push at me. I could almost hear audience members at my presentations commenting to me *what is wrong with you, given your childhood that you seem so right?* I was clear that happiness was not about a giddy state of silliness, but about a serious state of general well being.

Reading Csikszentmihalyi's book *Flow: The Psychology of Optimal Experience (1990)* had given me some of the philosophical bases I needed to support what I knew to be true. Csikszentmihalyi's whole deal is that we can cultivate a state of consciousness where we feel high levels of personal satisfaction. He discovered that goal setting, being "in the moment," and becoming immersed in an activity, yields a positive *Flow* experience. Prior to his findings I had no science, but I *knew* that when I was lost in a painting or when I submerged myself in researching those history books, I experienced a state of fulfillment. I knew there was something to that. I had also learned in my doctoral studies that when a person can shift from the left (logical) hemisphere of the brain to the right hemisphere, the creative side, a distinct mood shift can result. I knew that we could purposefully mood alter and that it did not require alcohol to do it. In fact 45 years of working with students who reported high levels of peace through prayer substantiated that.

I thought more about the roads to happiness that other researchers have hypothesized, like Martin Seligman (ReflectiveHappiness.com). He sees happiness in terms of three roads: "The Pleasure Road," like having a massage or enjoying a delicious meal, "The Engagement Road" which is involvement with family, work, or a hobby; and "The Serving Others Road" wherein one uses their personal strengths to a larger end. Seligman believes "The Pleasure Road" is the weakest path to satisfaction, but all three roads involve actions an individual can take to increase feelings of well being.

I pulled my attention back toward the pulpit. A vocalist was singing. I let her sweet notes wash over me and I felt a sense of peace. As I thought more about happiness I wondered, *why do I mostly feel happy?* I smiled a little smile to myself as I thought about this man whose service we were attending. How he always called out to me as I walked by, "Here comes Pollyanna!" He was being a bit sarcastic, but that was how he saw me. I have always been joyful. Maybe Robin was right. A lot of it is just in me, but I understand that one has to also work at it. I remembered reading a happiness research study of 4000 sets of twins which compared the identical twin sets with the fraternal twins and concluded that about 50% of one's happiness in life comes from our genetic programming. We each have some sort of as natural "happiness set point" A famous study in psychological literature, according to Kevin Ochsner of Columbia University, shows that six months after someone had become paraplegic they are just as happy as someone who's won the lottery! (Rock, p. 126).

Author, Dr. Sonja Lyubomirsky, *The How of Happiness*, says that "before long your happiness will creep back to its **set point** because of a really powerful and perverse phenomenon referred to in science as 'hedonic adaptation.' You know people get used to things." (*N.Y. Times, 4/21/2013.*)

I thought about this some more, about those I know who prove this. One of my heroes in life is a young woman who lives in the development behind our home. I have known her for 40 years, in fact, in my mind's eye, I can still see her as a teen racing her horse Tar Baby up the unpaved lane that was once our front street. Her hair would be flying and she would have a huge grin on her face as she and Tar Baby practically flew by my house.

In her twenties she had the privilege of being accepted into the Young American singing group and toured the world. Her life looked golden, but on the night of her engagement she suffered a life-altering devastation. She broke her neck and became quadriplegic. I have followed her life closely. Some mornings, when the dogs and I go out, we see her in her wheelchair on the trail. Always she has a huge smile and is interested in me and of course the dogs. She has made a new kind of life. She has a fulfilling marriage, a grown son, many albums of her original songs and her book: *The Last Dance, But Not The Last Song*. In spite of the impacts on her life, Renee Bondi exudes a sense of well being.

Another observation I have made during my travels, is that even in the most impoverished corners of the globe, I see contentment. On my recent trip to Laos, for instance, we were driving the long Ho Chi Minh Trail and our tour van kept making unexpected and uninvited stops in the most primitive villages so that we could experience cultural immersion. We would walk into a small village and see the pigs, chickens and dogs that live in the bamboo huts with the families. Little gangs of half-naked brown-eyed five-and six-year-olds would surround me. I loved it as their curious eyes studied me, and then I would pull out my video camera. That would begin the fun, as I took short movies of them and let them see themselves. There would be shoving and giggling. This was high tech adventure for them and they seemed to be in ecstasy. They made me replay it time and again. So much laughing. I could feel their delight and that of the adults we interacted with through our guides. Here they were living in the barest of survival conditions, without running water or electricity, yet I could feel their happiness and see their smiles. Perhaps it is merely acceptance. I'm not sure. I do know that when children have their basic needs met, their default state is happy. Of course in our fast-paced, high-tech culture which often fosters a "more, more, more" objective, some folks do seem to lose that primal joy and their happy-go-lucky inner kid becomes mute.

So it may be, that while some of us are instinctively happier than others, by making the right decisions, it is possible to grow more happiness. Why wouldn't everyone want to do that? I pondered that for awhile. I knew that vigorous exercise, for one example, caused lovely "happy hormones" such as dopamine and endorphins to be released into our blood stream. But it requires *doing it*. Hmm. I wanted to think more about that as the pastor asked us to open our hymnals. I would save these thoughts for later, but I became more convinced than ever that "happiness is a choice."

That evening when I got home, I researched more studies on "lifting your happiness level" and found again that it is Dr. Lyubomirsky who is the leader in this field. She is at the University of California at Riverside and has created some guidelines for lifting happiness. I was glad I discovered her new work because she offered similar tools to what I had been sharing all along with my clients, and before that, my students:

- Count your blessings.

- Practice acts of kindness.

- Savor life's joys.

- Thank a mentor who has guided you.

- Learn to forgive.

- Invest time and energy in friends and family.

- Take care of your body.

- Develop strategies for coping with stress and hardships.

CHAPTER NINE: PROFOUND MOMENTS

*"Only be careful, and watch yourselves closely so that you do
not forget the things your eyes have seen or let them slip from
your heart as long as you live. Teach them to your children and
to their children after them."*
Deuteronomy 4:9

And so a new world was opened up to me. As I packed
for my 17 day trek to the Himalayan Mountains of Nepal, I
could not believe that it was September and I was not in
school. It felt a little like I was cutting class. I enjoyed the trip,
which was marvelously energetic and culturally enriching. It
included ten days of trekking, as well as three days of white
water river rafting. We rode the small boats to our rather
primitive tent camp-site situated along the swift moving river.
For me, the culmination of this unforgettable sojourn was an
elephant safari through the jungle. I know there is not time to
share all the remarkable details of a trip like that, but I would
like to freeze frame something special for you from that trip. It
captures the flavor of my new life. (I hope you are not shaking
your head as you recall how freaked out I was about giving up
the classroom and thinking what a goose she was for worrying
whether she could figure out a different kind of life. I know,
duh! But I really was worried about that.)

So at this point our little band of trekkers was staying in
Chitwan National Park in southern Nepal when we arose at
daybreak for our safari. During breakfast on the patio at the
lodge, we could see the mahouts preparing for our safari. We
watched as four Asian elephants were slowly driven across the
shallow Rapti river. As we enjoyed that sight, our guide, Raj,
mumbled something about bathing them and would anyone
want to later? We did not know what that meant and our
thoughts were on the safari and possible sightings of rare two-
horned rhinos.

At the river we boarded dug-out canoes and poled across the water. By now our elephants were "saddled" with sturdy wooden platforms. I chose a particularly beautiful pink-eared female. She kneeled for me and I shimmied up her body, using the curve of her tail as a step. With a big pull I was on top of her! I took the front position in the wooden saddle and positioned my legs so that they were around the driver's shoulders. I noticed that he held a small hammer as he placed his bare feet behind her gigantic ears. *All the better to control you with my dear,* I thought, as I imagined the strength of an 11,000 pound run-away elephant!

Two of my friends joined me on this elephant, and the rest of our party mounted the others and we were off. As we trudged through the jungle, I got a kick out of our elephant as she surreptitiously wielded her wily trunk to sneak a quick snack of a tree branch. Her trainer gave her a little reprimand of a thump of his foot against her ear. She was a bit like a puppy grabbing at something forbidden. It was exhilarating to tramp through the jungle and view the wildlife. We came upon a rare sighting of a rhino family: a mom, dad and baby. All that was quite amazing but it did not compare to what was coming next!

The Mahouts removed the saddles and two of the elephants were standing in shallow water near the bank of the river when Raj asked, "So who wants to get a bath?" Without thinking, I raised my hand. Again, I did not know what this meant, but I was up for it. I was guided down the muddy river bank to the awaiting elephant. I was helped up on to her back and she waded into deeper waters. This seemed like an interesting adventure when suddenly WHAM! I was blasted by a trunk full of icy water! The gang from the river yelled, "Donna close your mouth!" I tried to close it but suddenly once again WHAM!!! She sprayed me again. I was screaming with delight and shock while trying to keep my mouth closed as I waited for the next blast! She sprayed me five times!! What fun was that?

Then she started to roll over onto her side and I had instant visions of my left leg being crushed so I scrambled off her back and swam to the shore. *Oh my gosh*, I thought. *How crazy was that? Who even dreamed this was a possibility? Who even dreamed this was possible in life?... I thought Raj said we were going to bathe them*...

My wet adventure inspired some of the others who waded out for their turns at elephant showers while the rest of us busied ourselves snapping photos and cheering them on. It was amazing, *but still, we were not bathing elephants, they were bathing us!* Sometime later, when we'd had enough, Raj again asked, "So does anyone want to clean the elephants?"

"I do!" I responded, again not having any idea at all of what this entailed. Once again Raj directed me to wade down to the elephants who were now lounging on their sides in about four feet of water. They looked like four big kids playing at a water park. One of the trainers ushered me to an elephant's back where I began to spread water up on her skin and rub. I splashed water up over her exposed back and nodded to the trainer to see if I was doing it correctly. He smiled and nodded his head yes. It was marvelous. Really, how many days in a person's life do you get to stand in a river in Nepal and wash an elephant?

I took a moment and calmed myself down as I wanted to really focus on this experience, as all that spraying had been wildly energetic. I began to notice the details of her body. I examined her thick grey hide which felt rough under my hands. The more I rubbed, the more confident I became. She seemed to be enjoying it. I waded up to her gigantic head and began stroking and cleaning her enormous ear. I massaged gently and she seemed to lean into my touch. As I continued stroking her ear, I studied her long thick black eye lashes. They were beautiful. I noticed a few graceful hairs on her head and noted a look of contentment in the visible eye. She was so huge and beautiful and wonderful. I could hardly take a breath for feeling the enormity of the moment I was sharing with her. It was something I imagine like being with God. She was still. She was relaxed. We both seemed to have moved into a kind of bliss. It lasted for long minutes.

As the others saw that this activity was safe, they scampered down the bank and began to work on the elephants as well. All of this lasted for perhaps fifteen minutes, but we were soaked, it was raining, and the river waters were cold. After a while, my fellow cleaners trudged through the mud and headed back to the lodge. I was still in my rapture moment at my elephant's beautiful head. Finally from the shore, Raj called out to me, "Donna, are you staying?"

That pulled me from my reverie. "Could I?" I asked meekly.

Raj smiled. It might be that he could see the expression that must have been on my face. He replied, "Yes." But clearly it was time to go back. I lingered in the water for a few more precious minutes and was truly soaking in the experience and the magic (sorry I could not help myself). The elephant continued to lean into me and I into her.

Finally one of the trainers waded in to help me to shore. I was far behind my group as I began to walk back to camp. After about ten minutes of walking I realized that I had no idea where the camp was. I was lost. I kept walking and soon came upon three Terai women who were gathering the morning crops. I think they could see that I was disoriented. They giggled a bit at my expense. I was after all a soaking wet foreigner, in a bit of a trance and lost. As they laughed at me, one woman gently took my arm and turned me around. All three women gathered around me and pointed me in the correct direction. We shared shy smiles. One lady even squeezed my arm in affection. Here I was half way around the planet, in a foreign culture being assisted by beautiful women garbed in colorful red saris, and they reached out to me as one of their own sisters; I, who was lost. We did not share language, or customs, but we did share a bond of understanding.

Poignant, short lived and beautiful. That was my moment with the elephant, water and with the generous kind hearted Terai sisters in Chitwan National Park, Nepal.

After that trip, I knew that I was going to be making the most of those "extra" years in my new life. And true to form, six months later, I was enjoying another magnificent river experience. This time it was the Jordan River. I had gone with Sandy and her church group for a two week tour of Israel. It was an incredible trip, almost like a journey through a living history museum. We learned so much as we visited historic Masada, floated in the salty waters of the Dead Sea, stood at the site of the Biblical story of David and Goliath, and explored the ancient sewers under Jerusalem. The sites were spectacular and historically significant, but they paled when compared to the symbolic ritual of baptism in the Jordan River. To experience that extraordinary setting was awe-inspiring. It happened to be a beautiful spring day as we donned our gauzy white ceremonial gowns and waded into the chilly waters of the river. The baptismal spot was lush with ferns and plantings. It was serene and ethereal. The experience was deeply moving in a way I cannot describe. I felt connected to something bigger than myself, to the history of my people, to the ages.

It was profound.

The last trip of that year, June 2011, was a big family African safari. There were ten of us, enough to form our own tour group: Donna and Ken, Julie and Justin and their three, Jenny and her two oldest girls. This was Ken and my treat for Megan and Jaycelin's eighth grade trip, but we could not help but include the excellent travelers, Jake and Jill. Jenny wanted to witness her girls seeing the wild animals, and Julie and Justin decided this was a trip of a lifetime and joined in with their youngest, James.

The two week adventure began with a pre-trip to Dubai. Ken and Justin were eager to study its architecture and economy while I was interested in the manmade palm tree shaped island that I had seen on TV. The kids were wild to try the famous indoor ski facility. For three days we enjoyed all of that. The children could hardly believe they were skiing in the middle of the desert on a 118 degree day, nor that they got to stand at the top of the world's tallest building.

The extreme wealth of Dubai was interesting to us. This was particularly so when the guide explained that the country has a big concern; so many of their youth have such great wealth they are not motivated in school, that they enjoy just hanging out in the air-conditioned malls. That was fascinating to us, as we tried to contemplate a country with a generation of young people who were not learning leadership skills.

From Dubai we flew to Tanzania where we met our guides and began our adventure across the Serengeti, one of the Seven Wonders of the Natural World. We had two big Range Rovers to use as we discovered all the "endless plain" had to offer. One day as we drove along a dusty road, we spotted three young boys wandering nearby. We stopped to meet them. Their faces were elaborately decorated with white paint. They were friendly to us as our guide translated our greetings. After we said our goodbyes, the guide explained that the face paint signified that they were newly circumcised. Custom required manhood training and so they were wandering for thirty days trying to survive in the wild to prove themselves.

Another day we came to a lion birthing area. We were able to get close enough to the mothers to hear their cubs purring as they nursed. From the safety of our vehicle we watched that spectacle for a very long time. There must have been some sharp cub teeth because every so often a very grumpy mother would hiss a snarling reprimand to her young. It almost seems impossible to be describing this. Seriously. We could hear the loud rattle of their many purrs. We could also see the cubs tumbling and chasing each other in rough play.

Most days we saw hundreds of elephants, zebras, and wildebeests. A common sight was an elegant giraffe forging for breakfast or an entertaining baboon picking lice off her husband. The Serengeti is home to the world's largest animal migration. Over a million wildebeests and nearly a million zebra, as well as other species, migrate across it. Truly there were animals as far as the eye could see.

Let me just share two more high points: The Leakey Museum and the Maasai village. We were fascinated by our visit to the Leakey Museum because it not only featured a whole lot of skulls which the boys seemed to love, but there was a fossil of footprints of a 3.5 million year-old hominid, the oldest such footprints ever to be discovered. Apparently the creatures had walked through mud and then volcanic ash buried the tracks preserving them for thousands of centuries. The Leakey family is credited with that find as well as some of the most important paleo-anthropologic discoveries of the last century. All of this was intriguing for me as I had the honor of hosting a famous Leakey myself. I met Richard, credited with discovering Homo Erectus, when he was a guest speaker at my college in the 1970's.

Just one more out-of-this-world share. Try to imagine what it would be like on your first visit to a Maasai village to suddenly have the women of the tribe grab your hand and lead you away. That is what happened to all of the females in our family. The Maasai women took us to a corner of the wooden fence that surrounded their village where they placed colorful beaded collars around our necks and cone shaped hats on our heads. Next they led us to a circle where we were to join them in their dancing. Maybe it was a courtship dance. It was hard to tell as it all happened so fast. The beat of the drums began and we were instructed to jump. The dance was all about jumping up and down in place with the women. At first we were shy, but with the encouragement of their broad smiles and laughing ways we soon got in the spirit of it all. The higher we jumped the more the ladies grinned. Justin, Jake, James and Ken looked on with a certain amount of astonishment as we jumped higher and higher. There was a whole lot of laughing going on between us and the Maasai. After a while it became apparent that it was the men's turn. James and Jake were good sports and jumped their hearts out. That was the social ice-breaker that began our fascinating visit.

After that jumpy experience, the tribal leaders broke us into teams of two and led us into the homes to meet the families. Stooping to clear the doorway, Jaycelin and I were ushered into a stick and mud hut. We quietly took our seats on a pallet-bed made of branches. As our eyes adjusted to the dark, we could see a pot cooking over an open fire near our feet, in the center of the eight by ten home. It was sweltering inside. Leaning against the wall across the way from us, was a young mother nursing her infant. Behind me I became aware that a silent, ebony-skinned young child was seated near me.

Jaycelin and I greeted our hostess as best we could in the darkness and with the language barrier. The young mother smiled. I could see her gleaming white teeth. I scooted back a bit on the pallet and realized that yet another person was also on the bed with us in the pitch blackness. I could make out that it was a teen-aged girl. I smiled. Using body language I asked if I could take her picture. She smiled yes. After about fifteen minutes of smiling in the dark to our host family, we were again ushered outside. The bright sunlight hurt our eyes for a minute.

When we met up with our guides we asked what was boiling in the pot over the open fire. We were told that it was goat's milk mixed with blood, a tonic for the ill baby.

The next visit was to the one room schoolhouse. About 20 children, from about four to eight years-old, met us with smiles and excitement. We stood quietly along the edge of the classroom while the children sang to us. One of the songs was in English! It was heartwarming. We shared our gifts of pencils, tablets and stickers with them. Their joyous energy filled the room. We seemed to thrill them and their happiness was inspiring to us. Later, we learned that the tribe teaches the children up through about the second grade. They learn enough math to barter at the marketplace. The elders do not encourage sending the children to higher learning in the towns as they fear they will not return to the tribe. As it is, using solar power, cell phones are making their way into the Maasai way of life.

Cell phones today, IPads and laptops tomorrow. Their way of life is probably threatened, but for now, for us, it was an unforgettable and lively visit to say the least! As our visit came to an end, I had my picture taken with the chief who spoke some English. He was smiling at me and teasing that I could be wife number eight! Ken was laughing, but I noticed that he escorted me back to our Range Rovers as fast as he could!

Our Julie has entertained us her entire life and this trip was no exception. All along when we would stop in villages or in little towns, the local peddlers relentlessly knocked on our Rover windows. They hounded us to buy their wares. One day during a stop, Julie silently slipped out of the vehicle. The next thing we knew she was banging on our window holding up a hand full of sunglasses as she said, "You buy?" When we fell into giggles she persisted. "Why you no buy?" A master of impromptu she had donned a floppy straw hat and her big green eyes were alive with fun as she continued to thump on the window holding up the sunglasses. "You buy? You buy now?" The more she hammered on the window, the more we laughed!

Clearly an adventure like this is almost a once-in-a-lifetime event. It was even sweeter for Ken and me as we were able to share it with so many of our loved ones.

For me, some of those funny antics are the most precious memories of all. At one bathroom stop as we headed to Kenya, I remember that Jaycelin conned me into trying some difficult yoga poses. As I twisted my legs into the Eagle pose, I began to sway on my one leg. The more I swayed the funnier Jaycelin thought it was. Soon she was in hysterics. Oh well. What is a grandmother for if not to provide comedic relief? As our journey came to a close, we decided that instead of regretting it was over, we would be grateful that it had happened at all.

CHAPTER TEN: NO CRYING

"People will forget what you said, people will forget what you did, but they will never forget how you made them feel."
Maya Angelou

December 2012

As the weather cooled and the holidays came into full swing, our family began to plan our Christmas Day pot luck extravaganza. Uncle Jim, Ken's brother-in-law, would lead us in Christmas carols, Julina would referee the traditional white elephant game which by now all the kids wanted to play. Our elephant game has morphed into a wild and rowdy event. Our main rule these days is "no crying" if you get stuck with a funky gift. We talked about the menu: Dan and I would each roast a turkey, Trey would pick up a huge Honey Baked Ham, and Chad was on pies, while others would think of new dishes to surprise us with. We were excited for this annual event which included about 60 family members. Across my adult life it has been important to me that those without somewhere to go on Christmas day be included in our party.

I was particularly happy this year because my mom was well enough to attend. She had been terribly ill for two years. It began when she had a seizure on a cruise to Alaska with my sister Sandy. Mom collapsed, was non-responsive for 27 hours and was taken off the ship in Victoria, British Columbia, where she was hospitalized. While Sandy tended to mom in Canada, our mom's 96 year-old sister, Jeanette also went down. During my mother's cruise, I was in charge of my aunt. When she did not answer her telephone, I went to her apartment and banged on the door. A faint voice answered, "Use your key." Since I had no key and she was not answering the door (and mom was unconscious), I called the fire department. They broke through a window and rescued her from her bathtub prison. Perhaps she had a stroke; she was disoriented and her arm was broken. She had no idea how long she had lain there. An ambulance carried her away.

I had to get to Victoria to help Sandy with mom, so Lisa took over with Aunt Jeanette and the hospital, while Sandy and I battled to get the Canadian doctors to release our mother to fly home. I had students, and Sandy had a dental business, so we could not stay any longer in Canada. After many days and with the help of our mother's most persuasive California doctor, we were able to fly her home, but only after we were certified on the oxygen machine and guaranteed that an ambulance would receive her at the airport. It was a terrible time for Sandy and me having both our mother and our aging aunt lying helpless a few rooms down from each other at the hospital. Our mother was put in quarantine and our aunt was given a feeding tube. Those were long dark months. Finally our mother recovered enough to go home, and our aunt was moved to a nursing home, and eventually to hospice.

That was all behind us now. This year the holiday season was a time to enjoy our family. Ken and I would host all our adult children, all the grandchildren, my brothers and sisters and most of their children. I was of course ecstatic. There is little that is more satisfying to me than having all my loved ones under one roof. This was something we looked forward to all year. That is where our thoughts were when suddenly our nation was sent spiraling into a terrible grief when a mentally ill youth gunned down classrooms full of small school children. We were left to mourn the death of some of our youngest citizens. In the midst of it, I wrote this letter to the *Los Angeles Times*.

L.A. TIMES LETTERS TO THE EDITOR
December 12, 2012

GOLDEN RETRIEVERS OFFER A MOMENT OF PEACE TO NEWTOWN

As millions of us sit dazed before the CNN news each day with broken hearts watching the innocents lain to rest, 20 of whom surely still believed in Santa and the Tooth Fairy, we are struggling to make some sense of this tragedy. The ugly truth is that there is no sense to be made of it. For the past 23 years I have worked hard as a children's advocate and I cannot still my mind. It fast forwards to the lost senior proms, graduations, engagements, weddings and baby showers. My heart aches for all the grandchildren who will now never be born, the joy that will never be felt. I cannot go to the mall without looking a beat too long at the little kids holding on to their mother's hands and thinking of the lost futures of the others. Mentally I was swimming in that sea of sorrow viewing the live TV coverage, when suddenly the big screen in my family room was filled with the sight of nine glorious Golden Retrievers walking across a grassy park toward the grieving people. My heart squeezed for a quick beat, for a strange moment it seemed like a kind of golden Cavalry had arrived.

The service dog handlers had driven all night, covering 900 miles to bring this special form of comfort. The light colored dogs were at their shiny best with coats glistening in the winter sunlight. The parade of Golden Retrievers stopped long enough for the media to share an introduction of each dog with us. The yellow tails thumped against the grass in welcome. After a few more minutes, the beautiful and calm canines were led into the waiting crowd, their yellow service vests announcing, "Pet me!"

Through teary eyes, I watched as little boys and girls buried their sad faces in the downy fur. I saw moms and grandmas bending to stroke soft muzzles. I glimpsed agonized faces turn to calm, if only for a brief moment. Absentmindedly I reached down next to me and stroked my own Golden Retrievers, Tessie and Zoe. While our national debate raged on over gun control, violent video games, and the lack of mental health options available to parents, my fingers worked through my dogs' soft fur. I know that healing from such devastations may not be entirely possible, but I will be forever grateful that we humans have the healing benefit of something as simple as being calmed by a gentle companion pet that has only one goal in life, to bring us comfort and peace.
My holiday wishes to you, Donna Friess

The television was relentless in showing the stories of the grieving parents in vivid and horrific detail. We kept the TV off. We pulled ourselves together for the Christmas celebration. It was lovely and I found comfort in the company of my family members. But the horror of that loss echoed in my heart for a long time. It still does. After so many decades in the classroom myself, I was haunted by the fact that those adorable little kindergartners were not safe inside their own classrooms.

HAPPY BIRTHDAY

As my seventh decade came to its conclusion, Julie and Lisa began making plans to ensure that my January birthday would be a memorable one. Besides we could use some cheer, the Newtown massacre was still echoing in our hearts. Lisa is an exceptional cook and decorator, while Julie is an amazing leader of fun activities. You put them together and I was given a party to remember. The event was held at our mountain home. Lisa and Julie made sure that Ken kept me out of the house on an all-day hike while the preparations were underway.

When Ken and I returned, we couldn't believe it; the house had been transformed into a candle lit fairy tale. I was laughing and laughing. Lisa and Julie studied me. I was beyond delighted with all they had done. I took in each carefully constructed detail. There were huge red crepe paper balls hanging from the ceiling, banners were strung across the room and tapers and fresh greens filled every corner. One area had been turned into a mini cupcake bar with each cupcake individually decorated. Soon our mountain club friends and more family joined us. A feast was served while Jaycelin entertained us with an a cappella rap song she had written in my honor. She brought her cousins in as back-up singers and they meted out the lively beat using plastic cups for accompaniment. It was positively enchanting! While a grin remained on my face, the delicate sounds of fifteen year-old Jaycelin's innocent voice brought tears to my eyes.

All of that could have been the culmination of the party, but Julie had a "program" in mind. She led a team game called guess the "fun facts about Mimi." It was pretty hilarious as family members shouted to out-guess the competition and try for the correct answers. The balance of the "program" included short speeches.

Rick was the last presenter. In his most thoughtful tone he began, "Mom, look around." He paused and looked at me. All eyes went to me and then to Rick. "All of this is because of you." His eyes scanned the room to all of my kids and grandkids and many of my loved ones. "Mom you need to be really proud of all that you have accomplished." I gulped. *Really?* I thought. It is not easy to find me speechless, but I was awed and humbled by all he had to say. There was more but what has stayed with me is the fact that the energy and dedication I have put into raising my big family and nurturing all of them has paid off. They appreciate it and they are good people. It is gratifying to know that my efforts across nearly fifty years have not been taken for granted, because a lot of what mothers do is invisible and behind the scenes. I took a big breath and smiled through wet eyes. Brother Trey raised his glass, "Here, here!" and everyone applauded.

That should be enough to say, right? Sorry, wrong. Remember you have been reading the story about our family and there are a lot of leaders. All evening, out of the corner of my eye, I had been watching Gracie. While Jaycelin and the girls were making their lovely music with the cups, I could practically see the wheels in three-year-old Gracie's brain taking over: *you mean to tell me you can make music with cups!* Grace has demonstrated a certain leadership style (some could say she is bossy) and so now you have to hear about what was NOT on the program. Gracie took over the party with an elaborately choreographed floor show.

While we were all sitting around enjoying each other in some quiet time after the noisy quiz game and emotional speeches, Gracie pulled the teenaged cousins, Jaycelin, Jill and cousin Victoria in as back up dancers while Megan was assigned the job of making music with yet more cups. After "making up the girls" which consisted of imaginary hair-dos and lipstick, Gracie was ready.

To ensure that all eyes and ears were upon her, she gave Megan the job of being mistress of ceremonies. Dutifully, Meg introduced the star of the show, the lead dancer, Miss Gracie Friess! Megan worked the cups and Grace the Break Dancer took center stage! She spun on her neck, dipped, leaped, and tried some moon walking steps and then more spinning on the floor. When that opening routine ended, she brought out the back-up girls. This went on for about twenty-five minutes and if the girls were not dancing fast enough, Gracie corrected them. It was very funny. Finally she invited everyone up. I am being generous, actually she pulled them up to dance. Almost everyone got to their feet. That or suffer the ire of our three-year-old director. The dance party began. Julie brought out glow sticks, the lights were dimmed and someone turned on the IPod. For the next half hour there was an enlivening dance party. What blows me away is how much confidence our three-year-old exhibits and what power she exercises. It is amazing. Maybe it relates back to being the last one. We all dote on her. Anyway, you can see what goes on in our family and why it was a birthday to remember.

In the weeks that followed, I busied myself with my life coaching commitments, thought about my next trip and about adopting a puppy. I often thought of that beautiful celebration which led to a favorite pastime of flipping through my mental rolodex, taking a minute to think of each of those lovely grandchildren. My teacher friends often teased that I had so many grandchildren that I could not possibly learn their names. Of course you know differently, they fill my soul. In chronological order: Jake, Jill, Megan, Jaycelin, Emily, James, Lauren, Ella, Allison, Katie, and Gracie.

The other night Gracie cracked me up. When I informed her that she was having dinner at our house and spending the night, she looked at me and asked, "Mimi you *got* pancakes?"

"Ah honey, it will be dinner time. Pancakes are for breakfast." I responded.

She looked me in the eye and asked, "Mimi you *got* French toast?"

With that I capitulated and Ken and I went to the market. We all enjoyed French toast for dinner even though Ken and I felt a little naughty about it!

Ken and I have been impressed and gratified to discover that all of the school age children are serious students, consistently earning A's. They are very happy people and good citizens. Our sons and their girls have participated in the Adventure Princess Guides program through the YMCA for years. All of the girls have enjoyed it, and it has presented an opportunity for the younger cousins to become even closer. The father-daughter tribes go on frequent camp-outs and have regular meetings. My sons enjoy the other dads as well. Most weekends the gang of Lauren, Ella, Allison and Kate can be found at one of the girl's homes or the other. All the cousins are great friends including my brothers' offspring, but these four are *besties!* Ken and I, (Mimi and Poppa), frankly cannot believe our good fortune. As you have discovered by now, a big piece of our lives centers around the family. They are our heart center.

CHAPTER ELEVEN: LIFE IS GOLDEN

"Happiness is a warm puppy."
Charles Schultz

January 2013

    With the holidays and my birthday behind us, it was now time to seriously think about adopting a puppy. Since Casey's death in September, Ken had been encouraging me to take action. I put it off due to trips and the holidays, but the perfect time had arrived. I began my Internet search. I was hoping to bring my new addition home in the spring. Before long I settled on a kennel which bred champions. The photos of the dogs were spectacular. I made some email enquiries and within an hour or so the breeder, a lovely woman named Linda, called me back. She was expecting puppies at the end of February. Perfect. I studied the parents and stopped my search. I committed to adopting one of hers. During the weeks that followed I kept my eye on the calendar waiting for their arrival.

    Saturday, February 23, was the birthday of eight beautiful one pound Golden Retriever puppies. Linda invited me to visit but assured me that they looked like little close-eyed balls of newborn. Three weeks later Ken and I made the 40 mile trip to meet the litter. When we arrived at Linda's home, we were sanitized, and after a get-acquainted time with the dog parents, we were guided near the sleeping pups. I sat quietly at the edge of the huge birthing box which dominated the living room. Chelsea, the mother dog, crept in with the babies. What a beautiful sight to see eight little ones competing for the best nursing spot. As I sat on the floor, the babies' daddy, Bumper, a big 80 pound Golden, came over and sprawled himself across my lap. I immediately fell in love with him and *knew* that I had to have one of his pups. As I stroked his broad head, I learned about his work as a comfort service dog in the local hospitals. His calm puppy would not only comfort me, but help in my coaching work as well, especially with the grief stricken people.

The weeks passed and the puppies grew. We adopting pup parents were encouraged to visit as frequently as we wanted, partly so that Linda could see us with them. As the pups developed they moved into a bigger enclosure and I was allowed to go inside and sit with them. By four weeks their eyes were open and they were wrestling and tumbling. By six weeks their enclosure was outside on the patio.

One day I sat down on the ground with them and suddenly all eight wiggling little fur balls descended upon me, climbing into my lap. You could almost hear them urging, *pick me! I am the cutest. Pick me!* They shoved and pushed each other aside. They scrambled to lick my face and burrowed into my lap. *Me Me! I am the best one!* You know I was cracking up laughing in pure golden delight. I stayed for a long time and paid attention to each little soul. All eight fit in my lap, but not for long. During each visit, Linda took photos of me covered in puppies. Those photos are treasures to me. During the visits I could not help but wonder which one would be mine. All along, when I brought up choosing a pup, Linda would steer me away saying, "We will see. It is important to see you with them so I can make a good match. I see them all day long. I see things with each puppy that you cannot learn in a visit. I will help you choose. Just be patient."

At home when I showed the photos with the puppies sitting all over me, of course the family wanted to know which one would be ours. I had no idea. *Be patient. Hmm.* I have not proven to be **that** good at being patient, but I trusted her and tried my hardest. The result of all those visits was that I became invested in all the puppies. I also came to understand that breeding exceptional dogs in not a business for Linda, it is her life's passion. Her greatest joy seems to be growing amazing animals who are intelligent, free of ailments and calm and then matching them up with the perfect family. Linda is her own Match.com!

Finally the day came when Linda indicated two little females that she thought would fit with my active lifestyle. "Donna, I don't want you to end up with a couch potato. Your puppy is going to have a big life and you need an energetic dog that can keep up with you!" *Well okay*, I thought. The litter wore color-coded collars. Miss Purple was brought to my attention. At that moment she was nestled under my chin. I noticed that she did not push the others away. She was relaxed. I held her upside down as I had been taught by owners of service dogs. She did not squirm. I was taught that this reflected a calm personality. Linda assured me that Miss Purple would be her first choice for me, but she had more takers than puppies and nothing was final. I was joyous to think there was a match, but since it was not set in stone, I tried to contain my excitement. I had travel plans, and Linda said she would do her best see that Miss Purple came home with me at the end of my trip. By then all the puppies would have gone home but mine. I sucked up any anxiety about which puppy, telling myself that all the puppies were perfect and that I would be happy; but in my heart of hearts, I wanted Miss Purple. Her name would be Lacey. I went on the trip to Croatia and Slovenia with my sister Diana, but a bit of my heart stayed behind in that puppy enclosure.

Diana and I had a wonderful adventure and I sent emails home to Lacey. Lacey did not yet have her language skills so of course these messages were in Linda's care. I mailed a post card to her too: it was a Golden puppy and it said *Waiting for you!* (Are you starting to get the Donna/pup picture?) Diana heard a lot about this during our trip. Two weeks later, Ken picked me up from LAX. With puppy on my brain any jet lag disappeared over night. The next day we drove to the dog show where Linda and her husband were showing their dogs. The puppy would be with them in their RV. I was not sure if my pup would be Miss Purple or another. It was kind of nerve-wracking. We found the correct RV at the dog show, which was featuring Golden Retrievers that day and knocked on the door. Linda welcomed us and we took seats in their patio. She vanished inside to bring me out a puppy, but the question was w*hich puppy? Will Lacey be Miss Purple?*

A few minutes later Linda brought out a sixteen-pound ball of fluff with a purple collar. As she gently placed her in my arms I knew it was *my* Lacey. She smelled me and her tail immediately set to its wild wagging as she began to lick my neck and my face. I was in heaven and nestled my face in her downy baby fur. Ken took care of the adoption details and we drove home. I sat in the back with Lacey, who lounged across my shoulders so she could look out of the window. We have been inseparable ever since. At home Zoe and Tessie welcomed her with open paws. My dog family was complete. Of course I still miss Casey, I feel like I am honoring his devoted spirit by bringing Lacey to our family.

You might think that is the end of the story. But it turns out that all seven of the other adoptive "parents" had experiences similar to mine. They became invested in all eight puppies as well and recently had a "puppy reunion." Lacey and I had to miss it, but it was the catalyst for a lively email exchange.

Last night at bedtime, Ken called downstairs to me, "Donna are you coming up?"

"Kenny, I am playing puppy. I will be up in a minute," I replied with my eyeballs locked onto a new photo of Lacey's sister Lucy, sitting on a boogey board in her swimming pool.

I have found great delight in this new "family" of puppy parents. It feels like we are "aunts" and "uncles." Judging from the amount of photos and emails exchanged between us, it seems the other "parents" are as excited about sharing as I am. This enjoyment is contagious and Linda gets all the credit, for she fostered a culture of caring and nurtured it. If you are reading this book to learn how I have been able to thrive after the devastation of my childhood, now you know another of my secrets. I play puppy. In fact I just plain play a lot. Our entire family is in on the action. Just last night I overheard this exchange between my daughter and Gracie.

Aunt Julie asked three-year-old Gracie, "So tell me, how do you like Lacey?"

Without hesitating, Gracie responded, "I love her, but not her head. I *hate* her head. She has an alligator mouth!"

We all laughed, if you have raised a puppy you know all about those sharp little baby teeth. They have fallen out now and our Lacey looks like her future adult self, only smaller. Her puppy days are almost gone, but we cherish them, even the less-than-perfect ones. I contribute to a blog *BoomerReviews.com* and this was one of my recent entries which depicts a day in my life!

Some Moments Are More Precious Than Others
Donna Friess

I am so happy there were no hidden cameras in my yard this morning for had the YouTube types gotten a look at a day in my life, I am certain that it would have shown up on America's Funniest Videos. I was innocently sitting at the computer answering my emails when I glanced into our backyard to see that our three-month-old Golden Retriever puppy, Lacey, had something unsavory in her mouth (well it was most savory to *her!*). I realized it was a dead lizard. Being the sanitary dog-mother that I am, I quickly got up to take it away from her. As I struggled to pry it out of her mouth, I noticed that our cats had left a half eaten rat nearby on the same door mat where Lacey was enjoying the lizard. I instantly saw that I had a multi-tasking challenge in front of me. If I did not utilize sufficient stealth, the puppy would grab that rat and take off. I maneuvered in such a way as to try to block her view of it as I pried open her locked jaw. Finally, I got the dead lizard away from her, but Lacey was faster than lightening and delightedly grabbed the nasty half-eaten rat and took off running.

I gave chase. Around the yard we went, her little puppy legs racing ahead of me. "Lacey drop that. Lacey, no-no!" After a few circles around the yard we were back by the house. She darted into my office and under the coffee table. I quickly moved the table to expose her. She took off again. "Lacey, no! That's bad! Drop it!" All that fell on deaf ears; around the yard we went again, big me chasing the racing puppy, forbidden treasure secured in her mouth.

Finally I thought I had her cornered under a bench near the planter. I got closer, sure that I could grab her, when she sensed my presence, she scooted far into the planter behind a big thorny rosebush. I climbed in after her all while commanding, "Lacey drop that!" All I could see of the rat was part of its tail hanging out of her mouth. *Yikes!* I crept farther into the flowers and bent low trying to avoid the thorns. I got hold of her muzzle. It took all my strength to work open her jaw so the rat would fall out. Finally it did! I grabbed up the thirty-pound puppy before she seized the bloody thing again.

I clamored out of the planter, placed her in the house, and got a shovel. While I carried the rat to the trash barrel I began to laugh out loud. *How funny was that?* And then I sneaked a look around the yard to be sure that no hidden cameras had caught a scene from my actual life with puppy! I let Lacey out of the house and hugged her close as I thought, *what a little devil you are!* I smiled to realize I had just captured another memorable moment. It might not have been a precious one but it was pretty funny.

Living with two mature dogs, Ken and I gave a lot of thought to the pros and cons of taking on a puppy before we committed to Lacey. However, as we spend our evenings enjoying the entertainment of our three dogs as they wrestle and chase each other, we know we made a good decision. It's a lot of fun, but it is also a big challenge. Lacey loves to drag the long length of toilet paper as far as it will go down the hall. She loves to chase the cats, dig up the yard, and of course she wants to bring us our shoes.

Across the past few decades there are some whom I encounter who seem a bit suspicious about why I seem so happy. Well, one of my secrets is the pleasure and love that I receive from my dogs. My new shirt says, "My therapist has a wagging tail!" Perhaps that is not so far from the truth. They warm my heart in ways that I cannot explain. They power walk with me, nuzzle against me, sleep by my side, wag themselves silly greeting me, and ride around in the car with me. They simply bring me joy.

Ken and I know that this crazy puppy stage is short lived, so we are reveling in it while it lasts. Oh dear, I hear Ken calling, "Donna, the puppy has a mouse in her mouth!".... As I run to deal with this puppy moment, preparing for another chase, I steal a glance around the yard, still checking that there are no hidden cameras!

CHAPTER TWELVE: HEROES

"Nothing is going to change, until people like you understand."
Maya Angelou

July 2013

Buddy, my granddog has been our houseguest a lot this summer, which means that I have been including him in the daily dog walking jaunts. I am so glad you have not been around to witness the spectacle of me struggling in the tangle of crisscrossed extension leashes as they wrap around my legs. Each step forward a small victory! The other morning I finally got things straightened out enough to continue my walk in peace and my thoughts flashed to the morning news. Nelson Mandela, South Africa's anti-apartheid leader and Noble Peace Prize winner, is celebrating his 95th birthday. To millions of us he is a modern day hero. When I lodged my own defiance campaign against my father, Mr. Mandela's courage inspired me. All I had to do was visualize him in that cell for 27 years and I felt stronger.

That rolodex in my brain clicked to another of my heroes: Rosa Parks. I have always admired her quiet valor. She *was* sitting in the "colored" section of the bus that morning in Montgomery when the driver tried to force her to give up her seat to a white man. Her refusal sparked the long bus boycott which ushered in a new era. That boycott ignited the civil rights movement of the 60's. Her single brave act helped to change the world.

Of course Rosa's actions pushed Dr. King to the forefront. In the 1960's, I began teaching my remedial English students King's *I Have a Dream* speech from purple mimeographed pages. I wanted them to master the use of contrasts, vivid imagery and repetition; to understand excellence.

By 1972, inspired by that lesson, one of the members of my class, an 18-year old black student, Jesse, brought in a recording of the famous speech. It was on a big vinyl record and it was a treasure to me. Now the class could *hear* the speech. Jesse became motivated and began to take his studies more seriously; however he struggled terribly with the grammar lessons as he spoke non-standard English. Conjugating verbs and the proper use of pronouns mystified him. We worked together. I gave him extra homework. We diagrammed sentences. I gave him make-up assignments. Finally he qualified to move up to the transfer level English class. Eight years later, with a doctorate degree in hand, he was hired as an administrator in our district. Over the subsequent decades, when I saw him, he reminded me of the turning point in his education: the day we studied Dr. King. And I never forgot his vinyl gift, though across the years I graduated to video and then to a DVD of the March on Washington. The march for equality resonated for me in a deeply personal way. Of the 13,000 students I taught across the years, probably about 10,000 of them learned something about non-violent resistance and standing up for what you believe, in my classroom.

When I taught the rhetoric of social movements, one of the stories I often shared was of me running as fast as my ten year-old legs could carry me to tell my grandmother my big discovery! We were traveling through the South. It was 1953 in Selma, Alabama. We were shopping in a dime store, W.T. Grant, when I went looking for a drinking fountain. I was so thrilled to discover "colored water." I was certain that it was a fancy kind of mineral water. When I found my grandmother, I excitedly told her of my find. Her face fell as she explained why the fountain was marked "colored" and it was not about any special mineral water. I could not believe it! Then I noticed three restrooms everywhere we went: men, women, and colored. It was a rude awakening for my ten year-old self.

Cypress College provided me with the opportunity to meet a woman who would provide a point of focus that would change my world view forever. She was author Maya Angelou, America's poet laureate. During the 1970's I was the president of the Artist-Lecture Series for my college. We brought in influential speakers, among them were Maya Angelou and Alex Haley, the author of the famous book and TV series, *Roots*.

Maya Angelou was our guest two years in a row and I had the privilege of introducing her and driving her to her hotel. I have never forgotten what she said to me one night as I drove her. Nestled safely within the cocoon of the dark car, the talk turned serious—to human rights. As her soft words washed over me, in fact, they still ring in my ears, she said, "nothing is going to change until people like you truly understand." I understood that she meant my fair complexion. I was young, in my thirties, but the recent discrimination I suffered in the faculty lounge during my pregnancy came to mind. Then I flashed on the physical resistance I put up against my father, my kicking and biting.

I understood what she was telling me, but it was not until years later when I *truly* faced my own abuse issues and went up against my powerful father that I began to comprehend the enormity of what it takes to win and secure any kind of human rights. Nelson Mandela faced it as did Rosa Parks, Maya Angelou, Martin Luther King and countless others.

Today, the six o'clock news is filled with the constant bloody unrest in the Middle East as citizen's battle for rights. Because of the civil war in Syria and the threat of sarin gas, I changed my plans to visit Turkey last spring and chose to go to Croatia instead. The trip included a visit to the city of Mostar in Bosnia-Herzegovina. I saw bombed-out buildings, bullet holes scarring city blocks of store-fronts, and destroyed property; grim evidence of the genocide that plagued the country from 1992-1995. Burned down homes gave testimony to ruined lives.

The Bosnian War was a brutal attempt at creating a "greater Serbia." Our guides could not even estimate for us how many hundreds of thousands of Muslims and Croats were raped, murdered and imprisoned in concentration camps as the Serbian army "cleansed" the countryside of its inhabitants to obtain more land. You know that I have been blessed to walk our Earth for 70 years, during that time I have been continually amazed at the counter positioning of human cruelty and human kindness; we can be so weak and so very strong.

As I thought about the side of courage and resilience, my reflections settled on some specific examples. I thought about my student Kerri. As a baby, Kerri suffered severe cerebral palsy. She cannot walk, talk, nor feed herself. As a child, her wheelchair was rolled to the corner of the classroom. It was assumed that she was mentally retarded. Left there in the corner, her keen brain gobbled up the lessons, and she taught herself to read.

She took all three of the communication courses I offered at the college. With the use of her talking board, she graduated from college, frequently presents speeches to legislative bodies and high school students, and teaches others with similar life challenges. She is a modern day hero too. In class, we would always know when Kerri had a contribution to make because her useful left arm would wind up and aim for the talking board. Soon the robotic voice would bleat out her thoughts. She inspired all of us in those classes.

One day she rolled into my office and asked me to come out into the lobby to meet her fiancé, Greg. He was also disabled. They have been married for three years now. I heard from her in an email this morning, when I asked if I could write about her. She told me yes and that I could use her name. I asked how she was, and as always, her answer was "great!" She is a very happy woman. She has never let her limitations stop her.

Geri Jewel, who also has cerebral palsy, came to national attention as the first TV actor with a serious disability. She played Cousin Geri in the sitcom *Facts of Life,* and has authored two award winning books. But before all that fame, Geri enrolled in my public speaking class. After the first assignment, she dropped. I always wondered what had gone wrong. I worried that maybe I had offended her somehow. I saw her a few years ago when she was honored by my college as Alumnae of the Year. She greeted me with a big hug. Clearly she remembered me, so it was my chance to use my words and I asked that question. Her answer: "Why Donna, you videotaped us! That was the first time I had ever *seen* cerebral palsy. It was such a shock to me that I dropped." Laughing, she continued, "You can see that I got over it!" Geri has been a pioneer in shattering misconceptions about disabled people and opening doors for them. Her story of dropping my class is also an example of how easily each of us can take something that is *not* about ourselves and make it so.

As the dogs and I headed back to the house, I thought about two other students who are heroes of a different kind: Luis and Mason, both originals.

Let me tell you about Luis first. He was a stand-out in public speaking class telling us about gang life and jumping out of the gang. For three minutes he had to endure a brutal life-threatening beating by several of the most dangerous gang members. We in the class remained silent as we could barely comprehend what we were hearing. In another speech Luis taught about Mexican wedding traditions. He wore a brown zootsuit and played a home movie. I will never forget that film. It was of him and his low-rider friends hopping and jumping their big muscle cars in a celebratory greeting as the bride and groom exited the church. It was a wild sight in the movie, all those hopping cars; I can only imagine what it was like in person! Luis was brave enough to leave the gang. He pushed hard with his studies.

A few years ago he came to see me. He brought his beautiful wife and baby daughter into my office. I could see that he was hungry for my approval. Of course I was elated to meet his family and see him again. After hugs and oohs and ahs over the baby girl, Luis looked at me with solemn intensity. He reached into his pocket and presented his business card. He continued to watch me carefully as I read "Attorney at Law, UCLA Law School Graduate.

"Really? I thought, *from gang banger to attorney. The power of the community college to change lives!* I was blown away with pride. He had done a complete one-eighty and I know he is helping others. Luis represents another kind of inspiration. He risked his life to turn away from the deadly path he had been on.

Now for my other hero-student, Mason. It was the fall of 1975. Following his draft orders, Mason fought in Viet Nam where he sustained severe spinal injuries, leaving him immobilized on a gurney. Each day his wife rolled his gurney into class where he was a rapt student. He was determined to complete his education and enter a career where he could support his wife and three children. The Viet Nam War was unpopular and Mason shared stories of being spat upon in public, a reward for his service. We learned of his deep humiliation, but even with the injury and the disrespect he received at home in America, he never gave up.

Mason's experience, and that of many more of my veteran students, brought the atrocities of war more intimately to my awareness. In more recent years when the Desert Storm and then Iraq War veterans would present speeches to my classes, war became vivid once again.

During one dramatic demonstration speech, two of the vets in class teamed up for their presentation. They turned out the lights and then began shouting signals out to each other as we sat in the dark. It was intense as the two young men simulated a war scene in our classroom. The shouts continued. They were showing us how to clear a building of I.E.D.'s, improvised explosive devices. When the lights were finally turned on we saw that the soldiers had tied ropes to each other's waists for security as they literally crawled through the space looking for explosives. They concluded by sharing how many of their friends were killed or injured. Harsh lessons. More than the lesson, was the reality of sending our own innocent young men to their deaths, sometimes for uncertain causes. I thought of the 4000 plus American troops lost in Iraq as they searched for "weapons of mass destruction."

As I returned home from my walk, more thoughts of Viet Nam and another personal hero screened across my mind. I thought warmly about John Dahlem. A decorated Viet Nam veteran, high school pal, doctoral classmate, high school principal and part of the oldest father-son team ever to summit Mount Everest. He and his son Ryan accomplished their victory in a storm in May of 2010. Their determination and fortitude to achieve such a feat boggles my mind. When Ken and I try to compliment John on his over-all amazingness, he always turns it around to congratulate us on some athletic event that we have completed. (Like a marathon could compare to climbing Everest!) He is modest, determined and courageous.

One evening Ken and I attended a talk presented by John and Ryan. They played the video of John at the summit of Everest. It was so emotionally powerful that I have not forgotten it. You can see it on YouTube if you like. It offers a glimpse into the kind of fortitude that it took to finish that climb. They have inspired me to do more, to spread my wings further. I admit my Everest moment was from a comfortable airplane seat in a flyover, but I think they are the reason that I had enough confidence to tour Southeast Asia by myself last fall.

As I prepared for the rest of my day, I thought about the subtle factors which motivate any of us to try something more, to stand up against oppression, to knock at the glass ceiling, to spread our wings a little farther, to not settle. Kerri didn't settle, neither did Geri, nor John, nor Rosa, Nelson, or the others. They persisted. You must as well.

OUR INTERNAL CENTER OF POWER

One night driving home from a Womansage board meeting, my mind went back to scanning my list of heroes. I realized just how many of my students had inspired me. I recalled one long ago Monday night. It was the end of class. As I was handing back videotapes and critique sheets to each student, one woman looked at her grade and burst into tears. She had just completed her speech on dyslexia. She used a clever attention catcher; she wrote a sentence backward on the board. Her opening statement explained that the way that sentence looked to us was how the printed world had always looked to her. She thought she was retarded, as did her teachers. Only in adulthood, when she was diagnosed with dyslexia did she discover that she was not slow. As she sobbed, I learned that this was the first "A" she had ever received in her life! I admired her. Even with the terrible obstacles presented by her learning disability, she did not give up.

My thoughts then scrolled to the hero-authors who taught me so much: Oprah Winfrey whose long presence on day-time television changed women's lives; Alice Miller, *The Drama of the Gifted Child*; Virginia Satir, *People Making;* Eric Berne, M.D., *What Do You Say After You Say Hello?;* Dr. Claude Steiner, *Scripts People Live;* Viktor Frankl, *Man's Search for Meaning.* I had to stop. Margaret Mead. The list would be so long. My thoughts came to the new neuroscience guys, David Rock, Larry Cahill. I really had to stop. But why, I wondered, had I not included Betty Freidan, Gloria Steinem, Kate Millett, Hillary Clinton or Helen Gurley Brown on my hero list? I certainly admire them. They opened doors. They protested. They insisted and changed the world.

As I drove south on the 405 Freeway, I considered the work of Gloria Steinem. In great part due to her efforts real changes have occurred in terms of laws and practices in the workplace. Across the years my respect for her has grown, but in the early 70's the angry, "women need a man like a fish needs a bicycle" rhetoric turned me off. A lot of those early feminists were too in-your-face for me. I love men and have never looked at them as the enemy. I was unwilling to cast half the population as the bad guys. I understood that extreme rhetoric allows for the polarization that fosters change, but it was not for me. Did the entrenched patriarchal culture need to be shattered? Clearly it did, but my heart did not feel the hostility toward men that the radical feminists exhibited.

Helen Gurley Brown's *Sex and the Single Girl* was a revolutionary book calling for sex and more sex: equality between the sexes. You know me, that would have been the last bandwagon I would ever have joined! However, her thoughts and words helped to free women socially, but that freedom had a difficult side effect: pregnancy. As an early feminist and longtime editor for *Cosmopolitan Magazine,* Brown had an eager following.

Five decades later it became clear that a cultural shift in terms of sexual freedom took root in those early days. Forty percent of births in the United States today are to single mothers, the great majority of whom are working class. Their struggles are monumental due to economic inequality. The 2010 census shows forty-two percent of single mother households fall below the poverty line of $14,500 for two persons. Twenty-one percent qualify as extremely poor, incomes of less than half of the national poverty line. There are over 14 million people in single-mother homes where they are food "insecure" and often homeless. The U.S. has the highest single mother poverty rate of any developed country. Clearly the gender-wage gap has in no way kept up with sexual equality. Reproduction within the financial security of marriage is more and more for the college graduate. This shows some of the ugly underbelly of sex and the single girl.

As for Betty Freidan, she gave a voice to the frustrations that generations of women experienced. I admired her and still have my copy of the first edition of her book. But those stay-at-home frustrations were never going to be mine. My grandfather was a frequent child care provider for Sandy and me growing up. We spent a great deal of time at the drugstore and with our grandparents at their home. Remember this was pre-television.

The tradition of storytelling was vibrant in our childhood as both of our grandparents were master storytellers. Through my grandfather's vivid stories, I grew up idolizing his mother Lydia. She died when he was twenty, but he kept her alive for me through his tales. A sepia photo of her hangs in my hall. It is the 1890's and she is standing behind the family drug counter at her 7th and Central Street pharmacy in downtown Los Angeles. If you look past her long Victorian skirt, you will notice her intelligent expression and her blonde hair. I was always told that I resembled her in looks and manner.

Lydia raised two children while working full-time as a pharmacist in one of the three family pharmacies. She was a pioneer who, with her pharmacist husband, gathered up what it took to begin a drugstore and moved from Illinois to California. The Southern Pacific Railway brought her to Los Angeles in the 1880's where she set up shop. I think Lydia was an unconscious hero for me, certainly an example of what women in our family did. Her daughter was also a pharmacist and ran that department at the Hollywood Presbyterian Hospital. My own grandmother had a rich career as a supervisor for the Los Angeles Department of Parks and Recreation. My mother held a similar position for 30 years. During my formative years, my mother was also the lead soprano for the Santa Monica Civic Opera Association. She was the star. On her side of the family, both aunts held down important jobs in academia, one as a teacher, another as a college Dean of Students.

In addition, and in a great irony, as the first-born child, my father was grooming me to take on the life script of "first son." Not only did he demand that I take apart and rebuild an automobile engine (fourth grade), build a house from the foundations up (high school) and understand the principles of the combustion engine (fifth grade), he also took me on field trips to the Los Angeles Courthouse to see lady judges in action (tenth grade). "Donna, you can be anything you want. You would make a fine judge. You could be a pharmacist, a doctor, a teacher." He was determined that I think "big" and restore the family fortune lost in the Great Depression, all the while being oblivious of an important fact. A child once enslaved in abuse who becomes empowered might one day stand up against the abuser. **The last time I encountered my father was on a courthouse "field trip" only this time he was in shackles and it was the Santa Monica Superior Court. He had forced me to become a judge. I judged his actions to be unacceptable.**

As you can imagine my thirst for these teachings, stories, and role models offered me something extraordinary. I was the recipient of powerful messages that churned within my young psyche. There was much fuel to feed my internal center of power, and as you know I took to the books very early on. If you have read *Cry the Darkness* you know intimately of my struggles against my father. You also know of my shame and that on one of the worst days in my childhood I imagined walking out the front door, crossing the sand in front of our house, and walking deeper and deeper into the blue Pacific until I was no more. But I did not. If a part of my psyche felt powerless to stop my father, which I truly was, there was another part, a stronger part that was not powerless and it resided within me. I heard a gentle inner voice, *Donna get up. Come on. It will be okay. Keep to your plan, Donna, and one day you will be free, you will be "normal."*

Sandy tells me it was God. Maybe. Perhaps it was the early combustion of my internal center of power, my secret engine. The psychologists call it the "locus of control." I have always had my personal Donna by my side. "My Donna" became a keeper of my soul. I could always depend on her. She takes up challenges even when she is afraid. When she wants something she goes after it with all her energy. I am purposely going to use the third person to make a point. When she wanted to become an accomplished portrait artist, she dug in 1000%, taking classes, joining organizations and working at it up to twenty hours a week for thirty years.

During the cabin addition, workmen dug up some of my earliest paintings. I know you are thinking, *wow, historic artifacts!* Not quite. They were rocks with colorful flowers painted on them. In 1972 they were the best I could do. Ken cleaned them up and reverently placed them in our china cabinet as a quiet reminder of my struggle to become a competent artist. I have published my work internationally, participated in art shows and won "best of the show" awards. While those little flowers were pathetic, (they look like primitive star fish.) They were also prophetic.

While in graduate school I took what was supposed to be "painting for fun." The art instructor told me I would *never* be an accomplished artist. (I will never understand why he felt compelled to tell me that.) I took my paints home and using Van Gogh's sunflowers as a study, painted them hundreds of times. I did not give up and I earned a B in the class (the only B in all of graduate school against my A's). I must confess that in 2010 when I stood in person in front of those luscious sunflowers at the Van Gogh Museum in Amsterdam, warm tears washed down my cheeks. Those were from the "Little Donna" who lives inside of me. She tried so hard, she wanted it so much, and she made it, but it took a soul challenging commitment.

When "My Donna" decided to secure her financial future, she dug in hard with Ken buying up rental units and then managing them for 50 years. That sounds wonderfully easy, but it meant nasty work-weekends cleaning up trashed apartments.

Remember I told you about my labor crew in the early years; it consisted of our three young children and some neighbor boys. The rental business was hard. It also meant enduring threats to our physical safety by irate, non-paying tenants. One deadbeat tenant's ominous threats still ring in my ears, "You will not know when or how, but I will get your daughter." Julie was just six years-old at the time and walked to school. It was chilling.

Once "My Donna" decided to see the world, she embarked upon at least two big international trips each year. Exciting, yes, but I often faced the unknown. I recall one dark and rainy afternoon in Moscow. I hired the hotel's car and driver to take me to the Park of the Fallen Heroes (today it is Fallen Monument Park).

The driver watched over me from the car as I silently strolled the monument-littered lanes of the park. It was desolate and unnerving. There were dozens upon dozens of bulldozed and busted up statues of Lenin and Stalin. Beheaded statues. Fallen heroes. Alone there in the drizzle, I was allowed a vivid reminder of the Cold War and the gradual demise of Communism in the Soviet Union. It also provoked my thoughts about global politics and individual freedom. The Lenin statues lay in disgrace, yet the day before I had seen his *actual body* lying in state in Red Square. There were long lines of worshippers coming to pay tribute. Odd ironies that I would have to work out later.

I did not want to alter my adventurous experiences, but they also contain an element of risk. They require that I step outside of my comfort zone.

On that same trip in 2000, the final round of the world soccer championships was being held. Russia was in the finals. The police were on high alert, ready for riots if Russia didn't win. Military tanks and troop trucks guarded Red Square. It was closed. I was on foot on another wet day when I came near the rows of army vehicles. My timing was perfect. There was no riot and I got to go inside. I was alone in the rain in Red Square surrounded by military tanks. A unique experience to say the least.

It had taken some fortitude to get there. I had to pass under the boulevard, through a long subterranean tunnel where the homeless gypsies and beggars were lurking waiting for an easy mark. Their intrusive words and penetrating stares creeped me out, but I walked with fierce determination and got past them.

When "My Donna" decided on a teaching career she chose community college. By age twenty-three, I secured my full-time tenure track position. For forty-five years I worked diligently to engage the students by creating intriguing assignments. I held "values auctions" and "sold" hope, wisdom, freedom, health, and more, in an attempt to stimulate them toward serious thinking. I used my imagination to make learning fun. A favorite assignment was to have them walk the "Red Carpet" where they would share for the "cameras" their take on some aspect of pop culture. Of course they were giving speeches, but it was so exciting that they hardly noticed. They loved it as we in the audience would whistle and stomp, simulating the excitement of the crowd in the bleachers outside the Academy Awards. Those were beautiful demanding years.

You get what I am saying. "My Donna" jumps in full bore and is not afraid to fail. She commits. But it is important to not get too carried away or to feel self-important. I did not inspire all of the students who came my way, nor am I able to affect change within all my clients. Some folks probably do not even like me. Some people enjoy their unhappiness and do not want to change. A woman came to one of our grief groups once and announced, "I am helpless and hopeless." Believe me there was nothing any of us could say that day to change her mind.

Many people just want to be left as they are. Ken tried to promote one of his best employees to foreman one year. The man replied, "Ken thanks, but I just want to put in my 40 hours, grab a beer and watch some TV. I don't want all those headaches." I think that is a life position that must be respected. In my work, people come to me looking for something, wanting to change. They feel dissatisfied, sad, hopeless, or perhaps unhappy. Sometimes we are able to hit a homerun, other times we strike out.

You have seen that I hold a powerful center of belief in my own ability. When I can convince my clients that they too have a **great power source within**, I see them take hold and embrace life more fully. I watch as they make changes and take chances. They expand out of their comfort zone. Not all of them. Some do not come back.

The internal messages we tell ourselves have the power to move us forward or keep us feeling stuck. Recently I have been having my clients play this little exercise with me. You can try it too. I recently enjoyed Marci Shimoff's interesting demonstration of this in a presentation. She is the author of *Happy for No Reason*. Here is how it goes; stand up and hold one arm straight out as you say "my name is Oscar" four times (if your name is Oscar use a different name, maybe "Mabel"). Have your partner try to push your arm down as you say that sentence the fourth time. Try it. What happened? It was easily pushed down, wasn't it? Now do it again saying your actual name and see if the arm can be pushed down. This time it was stronger wasn't it? Try the activity with your partner. For the second round say, "I am good at....." (pick something you *are* good at). The arm is strong. Then try saying, "I am no good at anything" or such, and see the power of the mind to strengthen us or weaken us.

The point of the exercise is to show the power of our internal messages. They can move us forward or not. While we are on the subject, if you are hanging around toxic people who think putting you down is a fun activity, you need to find some different friends. Negativity and depression are "catching." Our mirroring neurons pick up the toxic vibes in a millisecond and they are not good for us.

To my thinking it is essential that we strive toward personal empowerment and that we teach it to our children, grandchildren, and the youth within our reach. Life is what each of us makes it; we choose. I think it is essential that we choose happiness. These are important lessons. If you have gotten nothing more from visiting with me on this journey than the necessity of empowerment for ourselves and for our children, then I am satisfied.

I also think being present in our own lives is key. If we can inspire our youth to be engaged within themselves, to seek valuable and satisfying lives, then bravo, mission accomplished. If we can inspire them toward knowing that they can make things happen, then perhaps their internal combustion engines will burst forth. I felt in my early years, and continue to feel now, an urgency to turn back the powerful allure of drugs, alcohol, gang violence, and fogging-out in front of inane reality TV shows. It bothered me greatly that so many of my college students appeared at my classroom door feeling apathetic about their *own lives*! They seemed to have cultivated a kind of organic indifference.

Oh, one more idea. I like this iceberg metaphor; picture an iceberg floating around the seas of Antarctica. The chunk of ice that is **visible** represents one's actual **behavior;** what is seen. That behavior is driven by what lies **below** the surface: one's **thoughts and beliefs**. If the **thoughts** could be changed, there could be the opportunity for more positive results. It is belief in ourselves, (the below the surface thinking), that is going to empower us and the young people we impact.

How does one do that, you ask? How do we engage our youth? They must learn how to work and how to stick with something. Psychologists have shown in studies, that two out of three Americans have low self esteem, that we are a nation on anti-depressants. I am not sure I buy all of this. Regardless, what better way to develop internal power than to become competent? You can see why I struggled about leaving the classroom. I so often witnessed the internal change within a student. I could almost see the light bulb go on as he or she moved out of dark indifference to the bright light of empowerment. It was stunning! The news bulletin I offered was that *they were in charge of their lives*. While some could not even comprehend the concept, others jumped on it. I saw them dig in. This was NEWS!

You can see that my childhood experience set the stage for who I am today. I promised myself that once I became free of my father, that things would be okay, that I would be *normal*. I have achieved this, and I cherish every precious moment of it. I am a thriver. I am grateful for all my blessings; my health, my family, my brain, my energy, my clients, the dogs, the flowers and the blue sky. You get it. I hope I am not wearing you out, but the journey has a bit further to go. Let me close with two quotes: "The art of life is not controlling what happens to you, but using what happened;" and "The mind is its own place, and in itself can make a Heav'n of Hell, a Hell of Heav'n." John Milton.

CHAPTER THIRTEEN: OUR HUNGER TO CONNECT

"We make a living by what we get, but we make a life by what we give."
Winston Churchill

You know I love to stop action and absorb certain moments. This one was magical. I will never forget an ordinary afternoon about six years ago, when I accompanied my daughter to pick up her three children from elementary school. The bell rang and soon a great volume of energetic children filled the parking lot where we were waiting. Their excitement of being set loose after a long day in the classroom was contagious. Julie and I smiled at one another as the children raced past us, some playfully pushing at one another, glad to be free.

Soon we had collected two of our three. We waited. No Jake. The parking lot began to empty but still no Jake. I was actually a little worried, wondering where he was. Finally, we set out to his room. Perhaps fifteen minutes had elapsed since the bell rang. As we opened the classroom door a pulsating wave of excitement spilled over the threshold. I was stunned to find that the room was still full of sixth graders who were merrily working at their desks! More time passed as we stood there, and still they were not leaving. They did not want to leave. The room's culture quickly embraced me. It was comfortable. It felt almost enchanting. By then Jake had seen me and took me over to meet a key element of what was going on. I met Tank, a big yellow service dog the students supported and loved.

Tank was their philanthropic project. They supported him and one other service dog, Foster, through their class non-profit business. The class made and sold dog biscuits, plants, and dog houses. This dog business was to assist in their reading-buddy project with the younger children.

I could see that this commerce, the dogs and tutoring of the younger readers, piqued the sixth graders' imaginations in a new way, as it taught life skills. Jake took my hand and escorted me to a small space where the reading program took place. The sixth graders, using the service dogs, helped the young readers. Jake explained that research studies show a gain in confidence on the part of the young reader when the child reads to the dog. Clearly a lot was going on for the older students as well. He explained that there is solid science behind the positive effects pets have on human beings. *No wonder the students did not want to leave!*

Later that semester I had the opportunity to present one of my adventure programs to the class, which gave me a chance to observe what else went on in that classroom. I saw a teacher, Mrs. Benowitz, who treats her students like adults. There was a snack–cocoa corner equipped with a microwave oven. The students were free to make themselves snacks and move around the room. It was like no elementary school class I had ever visited. I could see she was not only turning students on to learning but she was also infusing them with self control and respect. It was awesome.

In fact it excited me so much that I created a portrait of one of the dogs as a gift to the teacher. When Jake's younger brother, James, had her class four years later, I got to see her again at open house. The painting hung prominently on the wall and it was obvious that she had yet another classroom full of students who did not want to leave!

The point of this story is the power of our human connections. Mrs. Benowitz knows how to relate to those young people. She uses her imagination and she understands the power of positive human interactions. She sees her students as people.

***

One year I had an epiphany. It was the last day of school for the summer. I picked up our dry cleaning at the cleaners near campus and said goodbye to the counter lady. She came out from behind the counter to hug me goodbye. That was nice.

When I got back near our home, I still needed to drop off our cleaning for the next week, so I went to the "home" cleaners where I had not been since school had started nine months before. I walked in, the owner looked up, saw me and broke into a smile. He had so much to tell me! His friend had written a book about "the children of the dust," the Vietnamese-American orphans left from the war. He knew I would be interested. I was. I listened.

At home that evening, I was telling Ken about my cleaners adventures when a truth of the human condition hit me. It was a big "aha" for me. In a long and clear moment I saw something about our human needs. *I saw our hunger to be recognized by others.* People know that I *see* them not as anonymous clerks behind a counter, but as people.

I hold that understanding and see it everywhere I go. One night, I had to have a key made at Home Depot while Ken searched the innards of the store for some building materials. As the twenty-something Latino made my key, I could not help but notice the colorful tattoos all over his arm. Having spent much of my life with students, many of whom sported their share of ink, I knew how important their tattoos were to them. All I said was, "Hey, nice work there on your arm." I meant it. As soon as he completed the key, he turned to face me, rolled up both sleeves, put his arms together to show that they created a painting of a bible story, his mother's favorite. His entire demeanor changed. He seemed to light up from inside.

As we talked about the parable on his arms, I felt a warmth enter my being, simply due to his genuine appreciation that I had *seen* him. That said it all. That was the end of the interaction, but the point is, if we can understand this deep hunger, and if we care to reach out to others, they open like flowers.

Psychologists would explain that many people are "stroke starved," especially those of us who come from difficult beginnings. We are hungry to be seen. By acknowledging others in a positive way we have the opportunity to benefit them as we fulfill our own hunger.

If you are in doubt about this, think for a minute about the phenomenon of Facebook. It now has one billion subscribers across the world with no end in sight. It is testimony to this yearning to connect. Your cell phone can have "live streaming" so you can know what your friends are doing and thinking 24/7! For me that is a bit too much information, but if the fact of something such as "live streaming" does not reveal this deep hunger, I do not know what does.

Remember earlier when we talked about psychologists thinking that one in three Americans suffer low self esteem, that we may be a nation on antidepressants? It seems to me we could go a long way toward remediating that condition through more positive interactions with others. I do not mean banal puff balls of inconsequential positive reinforcements, such as a child getting a blue ribbon for a fine bowel movement, no, I mean real positive reinforcement, so that at a child's core he or she knows they are of value.

One semester our class was on the topic of corporal punishment. I asked how many in the class had been frequently and physically struck as children. All but one student raised their hands. That one student happened to be my colleague, Joe's son. I was proud of Joe and his wife. So many children are raised through angry tantrums and are called vile names. I know that Ken and I were. Terrible hurtful names. Ken grew up being called "lard ass" and "Melvin" by his drunken step-father. Our father's favorite epitaph was "shit for brains," a phrase he frequently attributed to his children. I may be overly sensitized to life's hardships, and perhaps my grief work exacerbates the fact, but I believe in my heart that many people are hurting deep within. (I recall that Gloria Steinem described her inner landscape as an arid wasteland). I think that we could make the world a kinder place if we understand this hunger and act on it. It may sound corny, the "random acts of kindness" idea, but I know it works.

Often I will compliment someone and they'll respond, "You made my day!" I cannot believe that. A simple compliment can make someone's entire day! A casual acquaintance told me this story yesterday. It seems a high school boy, maybe a 10th grader who was badly bullied, was walking outside of his high school with his arms loaded with all the books from his locker, when he tripped and dropped the books. An older student, a football player, stopped and helped him load the books back into his arms. Later the younger boy wrote about it. It seems he had cleaned out his locker because he was going home to commit suicide. He felt hopeless from the bullying and the anonymity of his life. The older student's gesture convinced him he was of value. That simple act truly saved the young man's life.

Each of us is a story. The outside cover of our "book" may not be a true representation of the story inside. Sarcastic and prickly, that may just be a cover up. If you know someone who claims to be "fiercely independent," do not believe that for a minute. It may mean they do not feel safe enough to trust anyone.

One semester in relationship class I was explaining how sarcastic put-downs may get a laugh, but that they are at another's expense. The other is made to feel one down, less than, not good. As I interacted with the class, one young man began, "I never knew that. My whole family is sarcastic. Everyone puts everyone down all the time. I thought that was humor. No wonder I feel off balance when I am with my family. I don't want to be around them. Holidays are a battleground. I never knew..." and his voice trailed off.

Every day I hear my clients saying that they feel stuck, lonely, alone. Symptoms of this hunger. I know they want to live a full life, but they are not sure how, especially the grief clients. All through our journey together, the topic of expanding one's comfort zones has come up and here it is again. I think we can help ourselves and others by taking important leaps *toward*. Shyness is real, but the rewards for reaching out to others are unlimited. There are seven billion people on the planet and I bet a whole lot of souls out there are aching to be seen.

One of the antidotes to life's constant challenges is through our important relationships. If your friends have dropped off, it is time to cultivate new ones and maybe to ask yourself why? It is a big huge world out there and it is filled with opportunity if only we can imagine it. If only we dare to take the chance: to see others. Mrs. Benowitz dares to have cocoa in her classroom and to foster a culture of respect. Her students do not want to leave. That older student dared to stoop down and help the younger boy with the books, and he saved a life. What do you dare to do?

CHAPTER FOURTEEN: A GLIMPSE INTO THE FUTURE

*On being 50: "I'm enough! I don't care
what they think anymore."*
Anna Quindlen

July 24, 2013
Avalon Harbor
Catalina Island

As the ferry docked, the morning fog was lifted to become another sunny Avalon day. Ken and I, along with Julie and her three children, had crossed the channel on the early morning ferry. Jill's boyfriend, Cory, was along as well, for our annual family gathering. As we disembarked I glanced up to see a little armada heading our way. Jill was driving the family's Boston Whaler with two of her sisters, while Rick was not too far behind in a rubber dinghy with the rest of his family. *How fun, a greeting committee*! I thought. After our hellos, Jill's boyfriend hopped into the Whaler. As I rolled my suitcase up the gangway to the shore, I looked over my shoulder to see Jill's long veil of white-blonde hair spilling down her bikini-clad form as she drove the Whaler back to the bigger boat.

My memory spooled to any number of summers forty or more years before when I was the bikinied driver with the fan of long hair falling down my back. We were almost interchangeable. It was a fleeting moment. A pang of regret mixed with pride. Pride that the life Ken and I carved out to share with our family is so wholesome and filled with joy. All three of our adult children and the grandchildren old enough to have an opinion seem determined to carry on the Catalina tradition.

I stole one last glance as Jill and the boat disappeared into the throb of the busy harbor. It was not regret, just a momentary ache for all those sun-kissed days when I was a young mom with five-year-old Rick perched on the bow of that very boat and little baby Julie safely tucked between my legs. Maybe it was a moment of nostalgia for the time when there were so many sunlit summers stretching out before us. *Not regret. Donna, it is her turn now and it has to be okay.*

Rolling my suitcase toward the taxi stand, I recalled a statement I once read in *Cosmo*. It was an editorial by powerhouse feminist Helen Gurley Brown lamenting how she felt invisible now that she was past fifty. I was much younger when I read that, younger than Brown, but her complaint has stayed with me. *Invisible.* Perhaps it was a driver for my long time in the classroom. It is hard to be invisible with one hundred and fifty people taking notes on your every word. A kernel of Brown's truth has niggled in my head across the years.

I am much older now than when she made that complaint. Yet only rarely have I had such an experience. Surely hers was the result of being a part of the glamour world, the youth driven culture of the popular media with its potent currencies of youth, sex, and beauty. Age is a deadly force against those currencies. I had an experience with ageism about fifteen years ago when an eager producer "discovered" me. He was determined to get me on the New York talk show where he worked. He pitched and was shut down. The end. He was told "she's too old." I didn't let myself care. My life was plenty full enough, but he was so disappointed as he thought I was pure gold. It serves as a reminder, and not a subtle one, of some unforgiving aspects of time's sweet passage.

Wasn't it just yesterday that I was almost too young to be a college professor? Didn't that faculty wife try to put me in the secretarial section? Through my rear view mirror of time I still see those early teaching years when I wore my hair in a severe chignon and tottered around on uncomfortable high heels—*all the better to look older my dear!*

The "invisible" editorial could be a cautionary warning: the power of youth and beauty is short-lived. In a culture like ours which glorifies youth, sex, and beauty, it is essential to see beyond their allure. They simply don't last and much of the time they are not even real!

During a 2010 Oprah Show, Aging Beauties, cover girl and actress Cybill Shephard shared an incident that speaks to this point. One day she walked past a newsstand where her face was on seven magazine covers. All she could think was *it is lies;* make-up, lighting, retouched. Lies. The other glam guests were actress Teri Hatcher of *Desperate Housewives* and former sex goddess Linda Evans. The aim of the program was to explore life as the beauty fades. The women made the point that looks do not have *anything* to do with how you feel on the inside. All that glamour and beauty are actually tricks. Teri Hatcher went so far as to have Oprah's cameras at her bedside when she arose to go to the studio. She took the viewers step by step through the "magical" process of make-up, hair and wardrobe to prove the point that none of us should believe what we see. The guests left the audience with the message that true beauty is on the inside and comes from knowing who you are and not getting carried away by the "fiction" of the glamour we see on the screen and in magazines.

Surely the alternative is not going quietly to our rocking chairs, rocking toward old age. I think not. I do not even have a rocking chair! I think it is more important to celebrate the fact that we live as long as we do. To *own* our age. In fact to *own* who we are. So to that fleeting ache for those long ago days when time was spread out so far in front of us, I say *how fortunate we are to have had them.*

My thoughts raced to Anna Quindlen's take on turning fifty. "I'm enough. I don't care what they think anymore." The outspoken Pulitzer Prize winning writer and mother of three has a new memoir, *Lots of Candles, Plenty of Cake.* In an interview I heard regarding this new book, it was clear that getting older allowed her a new sense of freedom.

I smiled to myself as my mind's eye once again saw my lovely granddaughter so skillfully maneuvering the boat in the harbor, the long veil of hair falling down her back. The privilege was mine. I took in a full breath of fresh air. I realized that I had just been allowed something profound. I had glimpsed the future. One day she will be the grandmother watching her offspring steering a similar boat into his or her own future. I felt goose bumps on my arms as a rush of understanding fell over me. *You got to make it to seventy and you have all of these rich and wonderful blessings.* I thought to myself, a*nd Donna, it is not over yet!*

CHAPTER FIFTEEN: THE POWER OF YES!

"I don't regret the things I have done
I regret the things I didn't do when I had the chance."
Abhishek Bachchan

August 13, 2013
At home

Our time together must come to a close. In two days Megan, Jaycelin and I leave for an exploration of the Amazon River. We plan to hike through the jungle, float down the river on balsa wood rafts and stand with one leg in the Southern Hemisphere and the other in the Northern. The girls are very excited about this adventure. I am not even packed and I need to organize the animals for Ken, but I want to leave you with some last thoughts. Do you remember the charming little story about the starfish? It is a favorite of mine, as it says so much about insulating ourselves from the naysayers, following our own heart, taking action, and the power of one.

I awoke early, as I often did, just before sunrise, to walk by the ocean's edge and greet the new day. As I moved through the morning dawn, I focused on a faint, far away motion. I saw a youth bending and reaching and flailing his arms, dancing on the beach, no doubt in celebration of the perfect day soon to begin.
As I approached, I realized that the young man was not dancing to the day, but rather bending to sift through the debris left by the night's tide, stopping now and then to pick up a starfish and then standing, to heave it back into the sea. I asked the youth the purpose of the effort. "The tide has washed the starfish onto the beach and they cannot return to the sea by themselves,"the boy replied. "When the sun rises, they will die, unless I throw them back into the sea."

As the youth explained, I surveyed the vast expanse of beach, stretching in both directions beyond eyesight. Starfish littered the shore in numbers beyond calculation. The hopelessness of the youth's plan became clear to me and I countered, "But there are more starfish on this beach than you can ever save before the sun is up. Surely you cannot expect to make a difference." The youth paused briefly to consider my words, bent to pick up a starfish and threw it as far as possible. Turning to me he simply said, "I made a difference to that one." I looked at the youth inquisitively and thought about what he had done and said. Inspired, I joined the youth in throwing starfish back into the sea. Soon others joined, and all the starfish were saved. - adapted from the *Star Thrower* by Loren C. Eiseley*

What challenge do you want to take on? What inspires you? It has been a remarkable journey for me to be with you. Baring my soul has taught me more about myself. I appreciate you being here with me, I hope my thoughts have given you something of value. On our venture, what has struck me in a powerful way is that our current life reflects the actions *we have taken in the past.* The life in front of us will be the result of **the actions we take today and from now on.**

My coaching work offers a constant reminder of the frequency of life's terrifying and serious challenges. We cannot avoid pain and fear. To be alive in the world is to face them and persevere. Remember these words of Mark Twain. "Courage is the mastery of fear, not the absence of it." It takes courage and resilience to face what fate hands us. It takes being present in our lives. Life does not "just happen" unless we allow it to do so.

My scary worry when I left my teaching life was: *what is going to happen to me?* Would I curl up with my books, computer, paints, and dogs, and *isolate*? It was a real possibility, but instead I embraced the **power of yes** and expanded my life. When invited to Nepal, I answered yes. When Sandy said, "Now you can go with me to Israel." I said yes. When Jenny, Julie, and Justin decided to join-in on the Africa trip, Ken and I said "yes." When the idea of beginning a Loss of a Loved One group flashed across my brain, I said "yes." The impact on our lives when we embrace what is outside of our usual comfort zone can be dramatic in the most positive ways.

You probably know people whose first reaction is usually "no." No is easy. There is much less stress with the negative, no stretching or worries. But the power of **yes**, while often stressful, can give our lives a turbo boost to heights we never dreamed possible. When I was invited to Nepal, I was not even sure where it was! Trek ten miles a day? Crazy! Now I can do half marathons with little effort.

I read the feature story in *Time Magazine* in March 2013 about Sheryl Sandberg of Facebook fame. As a forty-three-year old married mother of two small children she is number two in command at Facebook. She helped them go public. She is one who believes in the power of yes.

Running this sixty-six billion dollar company is not enough for her; she is on a new mission to reboot feminism to get our sisters to say "yes" more fully to their own power and abilities. She says, "We hold ourselves back in both big and small ways by lacking self-confidence, by not raising our hands, by pulling back when we should be leaning in."

Leaning in is saying "yes." There is more. She gets it about *not* trying to be perfect. She goes for what she calls "sustainability." Doing an adequate job on the small things so that she can excel at the larger, more important ones. She has learned to delegate. Her children make their own breakfast and prepare their brown bag lunches. They pitch in, which empowers them.

I appreciate her honesty about this, because the only way I could manage raising our children and my career was through a shared effort with the kids, and letting go of trying to "be perfect!" And along the way, our children learned the value of both work and being flexible.

When Julie was a one-year-old in her highchair flinging anything that came her way onto the floor, plastic toys, banana slices, her dish, her cup, I would sigh and clean up. I remember looking at the dinner table littered with soiled porcelain plates, bowls, and glasses, all waiting to be washed. I saw dirty pans on the stove, the baby with food in her hair and on her clothes. It was then that I realized I had to change my habits. From that night forward I began to use paper plates. Perfect? Not at all. Practical? Yup. Sustainable? Yup. Martha Stewartish? Nope. But letting up on myself on the small things allowed me the freedom and energy to pursue other aspects of life. Maybe the energy I had to paint all those sunflowers in the beginning was stolen from my washing porcelain dishes time? Perhaps I was my own starfish that I threw back into the sea, and allowed myself to *thrive* instead of being perfect?

Remember back when we talked about those cornerstones to my new life? Well those principles can be part of your life as well. In my coaching classes one of the early assignments is for each participant to gauge how full their Happiness Tank is in terms of: Social Needs, Physical Needs, Spiritual Needs and Mental Needs. Many tell me their tank is running very low. The awareness of that fact alone can bring change in your heart. How full is *your* Happiness Tank? If it is not brimming over with affection, peace, adventure, exercise, loving relationships, and pure delight in life's precious moments, then now is the time to get that tank up to FULL.

What are the cornerstones to your life? As you might recall, my cornerstones were about Making New Friends and Connections, Physical Activity, Mental Challenges, Seeing the world, and spending Family Time. I work from a mission statement. What is your mission in life?

I have to leave you now. But I want to make sure that you are living at your highest potential. I know about loss and grief. You know that I also know despair and devastation, but it does not have to stop us.

A part of me hates to stop writing as there is still so much to share, but I have to go. You do too. It is a big, wonderful, invigorating world out there and it is still *our time*. Some of us do not have the luxury of many decades stretching in front of us. That does not matter at all, what matters is that we grab life and squeeze every last bit of joy and happiness out of it we can. I hope that on that very last day, you will be doing something you love. Along the way, maybe we can offer something to those we encounter. We can make the world a gentler, nicer place for the fact that we were here. This is your time. YOU ARE POWERFUL. What *more* will you do with this one precious life you have been given? How will you celebrate your blessings? Will you throw a starfish back into the sea? I want to know.

I have to close now and dig out my passport. Let me know how it goes? I mean it.

My best, Donna

SECTION TWO: COLLECTING PRECIOUS MOMENTS

CHERISHING THE LIGHT

Eugene O'Kelly left us a legacy of collecting precious moments wherever we are. Presented here are some of my favorite ones.

"It is not length of life, but depth of life."
Ralph Waldo Emerson

Gone Fishin'

As you might recall I have committed to training for my first full marathon, thus giving me more time than ever to reflect as I trek across the long miles. Earlier this month, my husband and I lost a dear friend to cancer. My mind keeps returning to thoughts of her, on how well she lived her life; in joy and productivity, as she modeled excellence for her two daughters. I think her life was her lesson. I keep coming back to how important it is that we be ***present*** in our own lives, not on automatic pilot. In a way, *how we live* could be seen as our ultimate art project. Is your life rich and vibrant, valuable, and enjoyable? Is it full of color and adventure?

Last week I was training along the shoreline at Crystal Cove in Southern California, and several surf fishermen were casting their lines in the gentle waves and it reminded of another such scene I once encountered. Ken and I were on the way home from one of my presentations when we decided to stop at Carpenteria State Beach, in California. We delighted in being together on a sunny fall afternoon and removed our shoes to wander hand-in-hand along the wet sand. Far down the beach we came upon a barefooted woman standing in the surf throwing out her fishing line. Curious as to what she had caught, I raced up the beach to peer into her bucket. It was empty.

As I walked back down to her, we exchanged smiles. I noticed her wide straw hat, her radiant face and the fact that she was well into her eighties. Remarking on her activity, I asked, "Are you enjoying your life? That question might have startled her a little, but immediately her face broke into a wide grin as she heartily explained, "Why this is fun!"

"So did you catch anything?" I continued.

"Why I caught a rather nice perch a few minutes ago though I put it back." Conspiratorially, she whispered, "We don't like to eat them!"

In that moment I saw her key to happiness. She was doing what brought her joy. She was fishing in the warm November sunshine for fish she did not need nor want, just for fun. That simple incident highlighted for me a secret to a satisfying life. I think we need to find things to do which fill us up. This may require some changes on our part. By making the best choices available, happiness and taking care of ourselves can become a habit. As the authors of our own lives, I like these words of Ralph Waldo Emerson: *It is not length of life, but depth of life*. As I think about my lovely fallen friend, I take solace in the fact that she lived a rich, vibrant and joyful life. I hope yours is too.

*"If you don't go too far, how will you know how
far you can go?"*
T.S. Eliot

The Amazing Horse Race

When our family moved to San Juan in the early 70's, one of the only cities that still permitted horses, interest in all things equestrian was high. In true San Juan Capistrano, California, style the Fiesta De Las Golondrinas attracted thousands of visitors and enjoyed vast media attention as the last non-motorized parade in the West. It still does. Many western style events took place in conjunction with this parade. One such gathering began as an informal neighborhood cross-country horse race and became one of my most unforgettable life experiences.

The race was organized by locals; farriers, horse trainers, and neighbors. A pot of entry money was collected and participants began to practice in the weeks prior to the race. One of those enthusiasts was me. You must understand that I was a former beach kid, had only been riding horses for two years, and had not yet mastered the use of the saddle. I only rode bare-back. On top of that I was a school teacher. When the cowboys heard that I was competing, they found it to be hilarious. A joke. I was a joke; a novice horse rider plus a school teacher, a very funny combination to the seasoned cowboys.

The start line was on the dirt road in our little neighborhood of horses and stables. The first year it was a smallish race with most entrants being our neighbors and the horse-shoers. The rough four mile course wound through an uneven creek bed of dry sand, big rocks, bamboo, trees, and brush.

I went out each day after school and practiced the race course with my big Appaloosa, Piute. On the day of the race, perhaps fifteen riders mounted and raced. It was thrilling. I put myself up against real cowboys and horse people and had a good time. My husband, Ken, an experienced horseman, easily took first place. He was on my horse, Windy, a sleek Arabian. Believe it or not, I, the joke, came in second, much to everyone's surprise. We pocketed our $100 prize money and enjoyed the party afterwards.

Across the following year the story about this race spread like wild fire throughout the equestrian circles in Orange County. I dreamed of the next one and this time I wanted to ride Windy. I began our training weeks before the event. I noticed that when she heard me coming, she would begin to quiver. She sensed something big was brewing. I could imagine what she would have been like at a real starting gate. She was over 20 years old and had been severely wounded on her front leg when we bought her. I sensed that she held a fighter's spirit. Perhaps I did too. We rode every day. Windy quivered and I practiced my bare-back skills.

On the morning of the big event, I was shocked to look out of my living room window to see dozens of cowboys and riders with their horse trailers and trucks parked helter-skelter all over our forty acre valley; horses and trailers were everywhere! In the dusky dawn light I could see that they had come from all over Southern California. I remember thinking, *my goodness, these people must be crazy. They have actually trailered their horses here for this neighborhood race!* I learned later that they had come from as far away as sixty miles.

This time the race was more organized and the prize money was larger. Look-outs with walkie-talkies were stationed along the course. Perhaps one hundred well wishers and supporters comprised the crowd of spectators. I was a ball of nervous energy. One look at Windy, and I knew she felt the same. We made our way to the start line.

My heart was pounding when I heard the sound of the starting pistol. Bang! Some thirty riders took off! There was a great cloud of dust. The course was narrow, adding to the danger. I focused on the race. I knew Windy would not tolerate dust. Before long we gained on some of the other riders. I leaned low on her neck and crooned, "We can do it girl. You know we can!" Across the rocks, up onto the dike, we charged like thunderbolts. I continued my urgent crooning as we passed more riders. As we pulled alongside the horse-shoer, Joe, (one who had made a lot of fun of me), a look of incredulity flashed across his ruddy face.

Before long I was in the lead. Windy and I were flying like the wind, my hair and her tail, flowing behind us. Quickly the course cut back, down again, into the creek bed. Rocks scattered below. We raced on. We were heading to the finish; victory was possibly within our reach. Suddenly my pad slipped. It slipped a lot, down onto Windy's side. "Keep steady girl. We're almost there. We can do it! Hold steady!" I urged her on. I was excited but terrified as I envisioned myself falling and being trampled by the hordes behind me. I grabbed her mane, hard, and righted myself. We charged to the finish line. To the shock of everyone, especially the real cowboys and experienced riders, I won the race! Ken and Piute were right behind me in second place.

Later, during the party, the look-outs expressed how stunned they had been as I raced by. One man kept repeating his thoughts, "Sweet Jesus, it's Donna!" He said he could not believe his eyes.

There was a dark side as well. One of my competitors was so angry he failed to walk down his horse and it died. A harsh reminder, I had gone up against a tough crowd.

Now, more than forty years later, that memory is still important to me. It reminds me that I can do about anything I set my mind to; that it is possible to step out of our comfort zone and compete in new arenas. We are stronger than we think. Of course today, as a safety-conscious grandmother, I would never consider anything so dangerous, but what fun it was then!

"It is not how much we give but how much love we put into giving."
Mother Teresa

I Listened with Ears on My Heart!

Last week the participants in my life coaching class were sharing a success they had enjoyed during the previous week. One lady, a mother of two grown sons, reported that when her son began his usual long monologue of complaints about his younger brother, that instead of trying to solve it or minimize it, as was her habit, she told us that she listened with ears on her heart. Instead of following her old Parent ways she relied on her feelings. She said her son's response was immediate. His entire attitude changed in a good way as he saw that he was really being heard.

It got me thinking about how much more comfortable it is for many of us to stay in our "heads" or as Dr. Eric Berne would have said, to stay in our Parent State. In that know-it-all place where we probably give unwanted advice, lots of criticism, or withhold approval, we feel in control. But that sense of personal control must come at the expense of the others around us who are hoping for understanding and love.

Imagine what the world would be like if we got more into our hearts than our heads and really listened to our family members, friends and coworkers. Perhaps the angry daughters would soften toward their mothers if mother would just LISTEN. Possibly the controlling husband would have a happier wife if he would actually acknowledge her point of view. Maybe the rebellious son would stop acting-out if he did not have to work so hard to be seen.

When my kids were teens I taught them to get out of the "House of Should" and into the "House of Choice." I was trying to get them to stop going on "automatic pilot" and think about what they really wanted to do. As time passed and they would catch me doing something that my strong Parent State said that I "should" do, which clearly I did not want to do, my kids would parrot back, "Mom, get out of the house of should!" It always made me giggle a bit to hear their wise advice and it would snap me to consciousness. They helped to keep me in touch with my heart and not let my strong head do all the ruling.

In some of the sessions I offer, there is blaming of the economy, blaming of ex-husbands, bad families, and self pity for the difficulties in the lives of a few of the participants. If we could lose the "blame game," the "I'm too busy game," or the "when my ship comes in" magical thoughts, we might be happier. It is time to be accountable for our actions, to stop the accusations and the procrastinating. What if we examined our own rackets and ways of manipulating the people in our lives? What if we honestly evaluated our lives to see if we are stuck? If you are not experiencing the life you have imagined for yourself then the old behaviors may not be working.

A way to get on track is to become accountable. You are 100% responsible for your life. To begin, you could discover two or three of your most self defeating behaviors and change them. Starting today, you could take action to make your life what you imagined, but it requires getting out of the old comfort zone and taking profound action. You have to set specific goals with time-lines, and become a ruthless time manager who refuses to let others distract you. Now is our time. It is up to us.

Personally, I think we humans are amazing miracles. We managed to get born and live in this beautiful time in history in this beautiful place. It is time to let go of blaming others for our place in the world. I think it is essential that we become authentic and accountable. We are the only ones in charge of our happiness. Are the stories and words that you say to yourself and others enhancing or sabotaging life?

Last year I was finally brave enough to retire after 45 years of college teaching. I have begun a new career as a life coach and speaker. It is thrilling and fulfilling. My mornings are packed with horse- back riding, speed walking with a new gang of energetic women, yoga on the hill in Dana Point overlooking the ocean and the on-going love affair with my three dogs and six cats. I know that goal setting, hard work, silver-lining thinking, and reframing a situation into a positive, are tools that work for me to keep me happy. I also know that adequate exercise, enough sleep, and a proper diet are my essential foundation. I love this thought of Emily Dickenson's "It will never come again is what makes life so sweet!" I hope you will make the most of yours! I hope you will listen with ears on your heart and let the people in your life really know you. I hope you are being your best self for yourself and realize that life is fun!

"Speech is the mirror of the soul, as a man speaks so he is."
Publilius Syrus, Latin writer

Love Newfoundland Style

Recently, I had the privilege of taking three of my nine grand girls shopping at our local mall. I had thought of lunch, shopping, and a movie, but the girls' had no movie interest. I secretly worried that I could not entertain them all afternoon with just the mall. Well I was completely wrong about that as one accessories store took an hour! Anyway, weary from the shopping, I suggested we look at the puppies in the pet store. The girls were delighted.

We were enjoying viewing all the breeds of puppies when suddenly the girls spotted a black six week-old Newfoundland. "Mimi, Look! A Newfoundland!" They were proud of their discovery as they knew I had once had my own precious Newfie. The four of us stood spellbound studying the adorable black fluff ball when suddenly the clerk appeared behind the cage and lifted him out!

Is there a chance we could pet that little guy? I thought. I must have voiced some of my excitement because the young couple behind us explained, "He is taking him out for us. We are going to meet the puppy in the visiting room." I turned to look at them. My enthusiasm spilled over as I shared with them about my Miss Cornelia Springhaven, a dog I got to adore for ten years. They were hanging on my words.

"Hey come with us! Come into the room with us!"

"Really? You would let me?"

"Come on." With that encouragement, I followed along. The girls were off admiring all the other puppies. Secured within the visiting area, the clerk gently placed the Newfie puppy in the young man's arms. Time seemed to stand still as his wife and I admired the scene in front of us; a great big, tall, twenty-something young man cuddling a little 12 pound puppy. The puppy melted into his arms. We stared as he smiled his serene satisfaction.

After a bit, his wife begged to hold the dog. I offered to take their picture with my phone camera. Great idea! She then handed me her phone. I photographed the three of them while we chatted and exchanged names. They seemed hungry for my motherly energy and I felt a bit like we were in the hospital delivery room crooning over a newborn. I learned that they were from Mississippi, currently stationed at nearby Camp Pendleton, California. They had been married a year and were not ready for a human baby, even though they shared possible baby names with me! I sang the praises of my Newfoundland experience.

Before long, the shop clerk came back to check in with them. They did not say much, dazed as they were by the puppy, so I volunteered, "I would like to adopt these humans!" Everyone laughed. Of course I was not really kidding. There was something so open and innocent about these young people. Soon my girls came to collect me as the Sweet Factory was the next stop on our list.

I lingered a bit longer. The couple had decided to purchase the puppy. Not a small decision as he cost $2200. No doubt a large sum on a military salary. I smiled my goodbyes.

That brief encounter has stayed with me. I woke up thinking about them this morning. How precious they are in their youthful attraction to the puppy, their charming southern accents, how brave they are being away from home. I recalled the earnest way the young man, Kincaid, spoke to me. He told me that he would soon ship out again.

"Are you concerned about it?" I had asked.
In his beautiful slow drawl, he replied, "It will be the last time. The puppy will be company for Kendra while I am gone. I'm not worried."

"You two know this little guy may grow to 150 pounds, right?"

"We've been looking at Huskies. We know." He smiled at me.

I just smiled back.

My thoughts keep returning to them. They are far from home, the holidays just passed and they did not get to go home. They are alone out here in California, yet their attitude is so positive. He is not concerned about himself, for him, it is about wife and country. I watch a lot of news, BBC and World News, and I see so much about our forces overseas and the wars going on in the world. This couple has brought some clarity to me about the sacrifice it takes to keep our country safe. I am not sure I have seen our military through these eyes before; a boy, a girl and a puppy. I hope we Americans, while we worry about the fiscal cliff and banning assault weapons, truly appreciate what it takes to mount our volunteer military. We are sending our national treasures, our sons and daughters, our beautiful cherished youth, off to do battle; to lose limbs, peace of mind, and sometimes even their lives. This young couple is just the tiniest sampling of the dedicated young people our country has raised. I feel proud and humbled and delighted that the Newfie puppy can do his little part for this family.

What a blessing to appreciate precious moments like this one with the couple who was learning to love, Newfoundland style!

"There is no passion to be found in playing small, settling for a life that is less than you are capable of living."
Nelson Mandela

Life is a Marathon, Not a Sprint

Recently Ken and I were chatting on one of our weekend hikes and we began to share the memory of grandson Jake's first marathon three years earlier. Here is how the story goes and I have to tell you, it is pretty funny when you think of the loads and loads of advice the adults were pouring over fourteen year-old Jake.

Months before the Catalina Marathon, my husband, Ken, challenged Jake to complete the 26.2 mile event with him. Jake at fourteen, had never considered such an arduous activity and had his reservations. With both uncles and his grandfather competing, he was persuaded to sign up. When the big day approached, Ken and both uncles, Rick and Dan, enthusiastically advised Jake on all aspects marathon. Jake must have felt a bit like a deer-in-the-headlights with so many big men energetically initiating him into their passion for running.

The big day arrived, under cover of early morning darkness, the Avalon boat took the racers down the 20 some miles to the Isthmus, the race start line. Ken advised Jake to stay by his side so that Ken could pace him and mentor him. The gun went off! The race began! Jake took off and after an uphill ascent looked around for his grandfather. As his grandfather was nowhere to be seen, Jake ran back through the crowd of runners to find him. For about two miles Jake stayed by Ken's side. He had to walk, to slow down, to accomplish this. Finally Ken realizing that Jake was light years faster than he, said, "Jake go ahead, you know what to do. Just ask for help if you get in trouble."

Many hours passed and those of us at the finish line knew that Rick and Dan would be finishing soon. Jake's sister, Jaycelin, and I, stayed at our cheering spot ready to honor our four competitors. As expected, Rick and Dan charged across the line in about five hours. They felt strong and had a good race, but they had not seen Jake nor their dad since the race began. They invited us back to the hotel while they changed and had a snack. They were certain Jake was at least an hour or two behind them. After all, it was his first marathon and it is a difficult, mountainous one at that.

Jaycelin and I looked at each other. She said, "No. We are staying here. What if they come in and we miss them? This is Jake's first race and he would be disappointed if no one were here to cheer him in!"

My sons insisted that it was not possible. Neither Jake nor their dad would be along very soon. They pointed out that it is a hard up and downhill race, with several thousand feet of elevation. It is very difficult.

Jaycelin and I would not budge. We were staying. Maintaining our vigil along the finish line, we observed the racers as they came in. Ten minutes passed. We continued to keep a watchful eye to the finishers. More minutes passed. Suddenly Jaycelin yelled, "Mimi that's him!! There's Jake!"

We were so excited we could hardly contain ourselves. We were jumping in place and yelling as Jake, hardly even sweating, keeping a nice steady pace, waved to us as he ran by.

At the finish line, other participants were coming up to Jake and giving him "high fives" and calling out "You're a Rock Star!!" "We can't believe you!" Jake mostly smiled. He was not particularly out of breath nor flushed and he had just run a huge distance!

That level of congratulation kept up the entire time Jake was cooling down, as we waited for Ken. More back slaps. "You're a star!" "You're amazing!" On and on it went as celebrants reeled Jake into their culture. I, as the proud grandmother, basked in the reflected glow from Jake. The other racers could not get enough of him. It was incredible. One older man who had taken Jake under his wing along the course, went over to the stats sheets and came back with the news that Jake had won first place in his age category and that he was the youngest racer in the event!

Jake continued to smile and nod as he "high fived them back." I could see what he was thinking, *so what is the big fuss? There were 26.2 miles up and down hills, I put my mind to the task and completed it. Not a big deal.*

Another hour or so passed and Ken came in. He was concerned about Jake. Where was Jake? Was he okay? Ken could not believe the news that Jake won his age classification and was over-all the youngest racer. Ken just nodded his head in wonderment as he smiled and caught his breath.

To date, Jake has been busy with La Crosse and his academics, but recently, Ken put up a financial incentive for any of the grandchildren who cared to race in the San Diego Rock n Roll Marathon this past June, 2013. Only Jake and granddaughter, Jill accepted the challenge. Once again Jake sailed in within two minutes of his Uncle Rick. As Rick checked the time-sheets, he just shook his head. Smiling he remarked, "Jake I have been training for 25 years and I am pretty sure you didn't train at all. I know you were up all night!" Jake grinned back. He was wearing a tuxedo-styled tee shirt that said, "From Prom to Marathon" on the back, thanks to his clever sister. Yes, he had been up all night and, no, he had not trained.

Jill completed the event as well. Each earned a nice financial prize and the knowledge that when they set a hard goal they can accomplish it. I could not help but grin when I overheard Jake saying, "One's mind can carry one's body to unexpected success!" I love to witness my loved ones as they become wise in life. I have often mused that life is a marathon, not a sprint. It is so important that we believe in ourselves, and commit the time and energy it takes to make a winning life.

Happiness is the spiritual experience of livng every minute with love, grace, and gratitude."
Denis Waitely, author

On Puppy Love

Sometimes they come out of nowhere, those amazing little episodes. It happened again today on my morning dog walk. My two Golden Retrievers were leashed up as we ambled down the lane by our home, when suddenly out of nowhere, a fluffy long-haired black and white dog raced up to us. Zoe, my older dog, was on instant alert. However, as the furry ball rubbed against us, clearly oblivious to any canine confrontation, she must have realized that the wagging little thing was just a puppy. I tied up my dogs and bent down to properly meet him. He jumped into my arms, all wriggling energy and softness. He nuzzled me. Time stopped as I was enveloped in his sweetness. I buried my face in his long silky coat. After a while his owner came to collect him. It was not easy as he and I were locked into a puppy love. Stalling for more time with him, I asked his name, his breed, his age, and if I could have him. Of course I knew I was kidding (NOT!). His firm little body felt so yummy leaning into me. Finally I had to surrender him and continue on my walk.

I could not wipe the grin off my face. I realized that it had happened again!! Many of you know that I work with women in transition and those suffering grief through loss. You might know I facilitate a Loss of a Loved One support group through the City of San Juan Capistrano. In that work, I help others to steady themselves and come to terms with their loss or new status in life. I teach that happiness is living through one's purpose and collecting "precious moments." I understood that I had just gleaned another one. What could be more precious than a six month-old puppy racing to greet you and sharing his enthusiastic little self with you? All it takes to gather these moments is to notice them.

Last week driving to a meeting in Costa Mesa, I culled another as I drove north on the 405 Freeway. The sun was setting. It was dusk when I looked ahead. In the distance I saw two huge birds flying low over the freeway. I thought, are they pelicans, sea gulls? They are too big...huge wing span. As I drove closer, I could see that it was a pair of huge Snowy Egrets heading toward the ocean. I laughed out loud. I thought, where but in Southern California in the middle of a cold winter could you see giant water birds flying over the freeway? In utter delight I laughed again. How lucky we are to be alive. Part of the joy is being present enough to round up these precious moments.

*"What we pay attention to, and how we pay attention,
determines the content and quality of life."*
Mihaly Csikszentmihalyi

Trials of the Tooth Fairy

Labor Day weekend found our entire family at our mountain cabin. Our granddaughter Katie, age seven, came running to a group of us and announced that she had lost another tooth! She was so excited! "Wow! We all responded with appropriate enthusiasm. Aunt Julie asked, "Will the tooth fairy find you here?"

In a confident tone Katie responded, "Well she always finds me at Catalina and when I am on my trips. I think she will find me here! I cannot believe that it fell out while I was eating an Oreo!"

A little later, her 10 year-old sister Ella came in and announced that she too had lost a tooth.

"Oh no!" I said. "What is happening to your teeth girls? Is it the candy?"

"No Mimi. You silly. It is natural. Our permanent teeth are coming in!"

"Oh!" I responded thoughtfully.

Not much more was said about the lost teeth, as ultimate Frisbee was played, a contingent went on an exploratory hike, then dinner, and finally a big dance.

After the dance, everyone went to bed, when suddenly, my daughter, their aunt Julie, realized that perhaps her brother and sister-in-law forgot the tooth fairy. Julie found Katie's older sister Jill. In an urgent whisper she asked, "Jill did they forget the tooth fairy?"

"Oh gosh, I'm not sure. I'll go ask my parents." Jill quietly roused her dad who was sound asleep. "Dad, did you guys do the tooth fairy?"

"Oh no! I forgot all about it. Take care of it for me. Please." And he rolled over and went back to sleep.

Jill came back downstairs and reported, "Aunt Julie they forgot."

Julie frantically rummaged through her purse and found only twenties and a five. She knew Ella had also lost a tooth that day. She needed to find some money fast! The usual tooth fairy amount was two dollars per tooth. Julie ran around the cabin asking anyone who was still awake, "Do you have some ones? "

Jake, her 17-year-old responded, "Mom, I have a five. But it is *only* a loan!"

"I'll take it!"

With that, Julie slipped quietly into the sleeping girls' room. She bent down to kiss each sleeping girl good night and surreptitiously slipped a five dollar bill under each pillow.

She then came upstairs to where her dad and I were reading in our room and reported this little drama of how the tooth fairy was forgotten! We laughed and thought maybe by the last of five girls it is harder to remember all these details. We said goodnight and enjoyed Julie's little adventure.

Early the next morning, I awoke and quietly went downstairs for coffee. Katie was already up and had quite an exciting story to share.

"Mimi you won't believe this," she paused and took a breath, "but that tooth I lost yesterday must be my *lucky* tooth because I am seven! Guess how much the tooth fairy left?"

I paused thoughtfully to play her game. "I think two dollars."

"No, Mimi. It must be my *lucky* tooth. She left five dollars! I just knew she would find me here, but five dollars! I cannot believe it! What is so odd is that when I went to the bathroom about an hour after I had gone to sleep, I found the money on the floor near my pillow. Maybe when I turned my pillow it fell to the floor. It seems funny that the tooth fairy came so fast!"

This little vignette illustrates the sheer joy children are able to find in small events, and as adults, I think it is important for us to search out these precious moments when we can. It seems like when we are successful in appreciating the little things, they can string together to create happiness. I know they do for me. I hope Katie is not getting suspicious......

READER'S GUIDE: QUESTIONS FOR DISCUSSION

1. Early in the book Donna challenges you to bring your detective equipment and discover some of the reasons why she was able to move from devastated child to the positive woman she is today. A frequent result of father-child sexual abuse is mental illness, alcoholism, drug addiction, promiscuity, broken relationships, or serial monogamy. Many such victims suffer chronic depression, anxiety, and acute post traumatic stress disorder.

2. What were the benefits to Donna that resulted from her public activism? Why did she need to be pro-active?

3. Donna talks about Resilience and Human Hardiness. How is she resilient? How are you personally resilient?

4. Donna believes in "an examined life." When you think about your life, how are you like or unlike Donna?

5. Donna seemed to have a lot of anxiety around the issue of retirement from teaching? Why do you think that is? What big move do you want to make but for which you too have some anxiety?

6. Donna admits that her marriage has not always been easy. Why do you think she stayed? What were the strengths of her relationship with her husband? What are the strengths of one of your important relationships?

7. Why do you think it bothered Donna for so long to have her half-brother given up for adoption at birth?

8. This book has a lot of material on "choosing happiness" and one's natural "happiness set point." When you think of yourself compared to those around you, where do you think your happiness "set point" is? If you think of your own happiness as a "happiness tank," how full is your tank?

9. This book challenges its readers to step out of their comfort zones and live the most satisfying lives possible. Is there something you have dreamed of doing but are afraid? What is it? Discuss what it would take for you to do it.

10. This book describes some of the heroes who have inspired Donna, who inspires you? Who are two of your

heroes? What qualities do your heroes have that inspire you?

11. One of the most powerful goal setting tools that Donna uses is the creation of a "Goals Book." This includes pictures from magazines to illustrate: 50 things you want to HAVE in life, 50 things you want to DO in life, and 50 things you want to BE in life. Creation of your Goals Book is something to do across time. It might be fun to share with a friend.

12. What is the main idea that you have taken away from reading this book?

REFERENCES

Bateson, Mary Catherine. **Composing a Life.** New York: Atlantic Monthly Press, 1989.

Bateson, Mary Catherine. **Composing a Further Life.** New York: Alfred Knopf, 2010.

Berne, Eric. **What Do You Say After You Say Hello?** New York; Bantam, 1972.

Cahill, Larry. Psycho-biologist. The Cahill Laboratory at the University of California, Irvine. Lecture: *The Brain at Work.* Inside Edge: January 2013.

Canfield, Jack. **The Success Principles.** New York: Harper Resource Book, 2005.

Covey. Stephen R. **The 7 Habits of Highly Effective People.** New York: Free Press, 1989, 2004.

Covey, Stephen. **First Things First.** New York: Fireside Book Simon & Schuster. 1994.

Csikszentmihalyi, Mihaly. **Flow: The Psychology of Optimal Experience.** New York: Harper and Row, 1990.

Frankl, Viktor. **The Will to Meaning.** New York: Meridian Book. 1966, 1989.

Friess, Donna, L. **Circle of Love: Guide to Successful Relationships, 3rd Edition.** California: H.I.H. Publishing, 2008.

Friess, Donna and Tonkovich, Janet. **Whispering Waters: Historic Weesha and the Settling of Southern California.** California: H.I.H Publishing, 1998.

Friess, Donna and Tonkovich, Janet. **A Chronicle of Historic Weesha and the Upper Santa Ana River Valley.** California: H.I.H. Publishing, 2000.

Friess, Donna. **One Hundred Years of Weesha: Members' Stories.** California: H.I.H. Publishing, 2010.

Finkelhor, David. **Sexually Victimized Children.** New York: The Free Press, 1979.

Gallagher, B.J. **The Power of Positive Doing.** Illinois: Simple Truths, LLC, 2012.

Glasser, William. **Stations of the Mind.** New York: Harper and Row, 1981.

Goleman, Daniel. **Social Intelligence.** New York: Bantam Book, 2006.

Jung, Carl. **Memories, Dreams and Reflections.** New York: Pantheon Books, 1963.

Kurzweil, Ray. **How to Create a Mind: the Secret of Human Thought Revealed.** New York: Viking, 2012.

May, Rollo. **Love And Will.** New York: Norton, 1966.

Miller, Alice. **The Drama of the Gifted Child.** New York: Harper and Row, 1997.

Miller, Alice. **Thou Shall Not Be Aware: Society's Betrayal of the Child.** New York: Harper and Row, 1981.

O'Kelly, Eugene. **Chasing Daylight: How My Forthcoming Death Transformed My Life.** New York: McGraw Hill. 2008.

Rock, David. **Quiet Leadership.** New York: Harper, 2006.

Rock, David. **Your Brain at Work: Strategies for Overcoming Distraction, Regaining Focus, and Working Smarter All Day Long.** New York: Harper Business, 2009.

Shimoff, Marci. Lecture: *Happy for No Reason.* May 11, 2013.Women's Journey Conference, University of California, Irvine.

Steinem, Gloria. **Revolution from Within.** Boston: Little, Brown and Company,1993.

Steiner, Claude. **Scripts People Live.** New York: Bantam, 1974.

Tillich, Paul. **The Courage To Be.** New York: Yale University Press, 1980.

Weil, Elizabeth. 2013. "Happiness Inc." [On Sonja Lyubomirsky] *New York Times*, April 21.

Woolf, Virginia. **A Room of One's Own.** New York: Harvest: HBJ, 1929

INDEX

Mandela, Nelson, 163
MASA, 48
McMartin Case, 47
Millennium Bug, 80
Mindful, 29, 120

Neuroscience, 119-120
Nepal, 137-140
Newtown Massacre, 148-151
Norway, 70-72

Ocean Park Pier, 4
O'Kelly, Eugene 116, 196
One Hundred Years Weesha, 88,92
Oprah Show, 41-43,189

Parks, Rosa, 163
Power of Yes! 193
PTSD, 27, 48

Quindlen, Anna, 130, 189

Reeves. Claire, 48
Reflective Happiness, 132
Reframe Event, 113, 128,131
Resiliency, 113
Robinson, John, 61
Rock, David, 120-121

Sandberg, Sheryl, 193
Santa Cruz Boardwalk, 5
Seligman, Martin, 132
Shimoff, Marci, 178
Single Mother Households, 172
Social Cognitive Neuroscience, 49, 119

Southeast Asia, 122-124
Starfish Story, 191-192
Steinem, Gloria, 172,184
Stetson, Mary, 52-67

Tanzania, 141-143
Terrorist Attack, 9/11, 82-83
Tonkovich, Janet, Paul, 55-59, 62, 91-23
Train Brain, 119
TTAC Justice Dept, 48

Vertigo, 124

Wassailing, 53
Weesha, 53-59
Weesha 100th Anniversary, 90-92
Whispering Waters: Historic Weesha, 55
Winfrey, Oprah, 36, 41-44, 46, 171, 189
World Trade Center, 83-84

Y2K, 82